Revolutionary times, revolutionary lives

Personal accounts of the liberation struggle

Edited by Bob Myers

Index Books
South Africa Series No. 1

© Index Books 1997

Published by Index Books (Indexreach Ltd.)
28 Charlotte Street, London W1P 1HJ

Typeset by Sumner Type, London SE22
Printed by Trade Union Printing Services, Newcastle upon Tyne

A C.I.P. catalogue record for this book is available from
the British Library

To contact Workers International, write to PO Box 48764, Qualbert,
4078, Durban, South Africa; or c/o Index Books, 28 Charlotte Street,
London W1P 1HJ.

ISBN: 1-871518-19-9

CONTENTS

Introduction	1
The Story of a South African revolutionary	4
Fighting corruption	30
How SWAPO tortured its own fighters	32
'A place where you are going to sleep': a Namibian story	39
Meeting survivors	49
'Torture became a system': interviews with ANC fighters	51
A miscarriage of democracy: the ANC security department in the 1984 mutiny in Umkhonto we Sizwe	55
An open letter to Nelson Mandela from ex-ANC detainees	99
Challenging Mandela	103
'Nobody could walk free': an Angolan woman's story	107
Rebuilding the international revolutionary movement	116

INTRODUCTION

From different places, from different backgrounds, travelling down different roads of struggle, the people from South Africa, Namibia and Angola whose articles are in this book have all worked to build organisations capable of transforming society and freeing the people of Africa from oppression and the African continent from its position as a plundered continent. Their separate lives and separate struggles have crossed and become connected as they have found that the problems they face are common to them all.

I grew up in London, far from the kind of existence which these writers experienced, but even as a young boy I remember seeing the newspaper pictures of the Sharpeville massacre. As a teenager I began to learn about, and hate, apartheid. When the whites in Rhodesia made their unilateral declaration of independence (UDI) rather than concede black majority rule, I took my first political stand: sticking a printed slogan on my school bag — 'One man, one vote' (my brother, older and more radical, wanted me to cross out 'vote' and put 'gun'). Over the next 20 years I followed the development of the great political movements in Southern Africa. The year 1985 marked a sudden change in my relationship with those struggles. In that year South Africa was engulfed in the revolt of the township youth, and every night our television news was filled with scenes of their fight against apartheid. Coinciding with that was an eruption in the Workers Revolutionary Party of which I had been

2   REVOLUTIONARY TIMES, REVOLUTIONARY LIVES

a member for many years. A revolt of the party's members against a bureaucratic leadership and a sect-like existence suddenly freed us from a daily routine of robotic newspaper-selling and mindless adherence to the party 'line' which had walled us off from involvement in any activity outside the strictly defined 'party building'.

Relishing this new 'freedom' of action and thought, I became involved in the non-stop picket outside the South African Embassy in London. For three years, night and day, people stood, sang, slept and demonstrated outside the embassy, demanding the release of all political prisoners. From being a distant observer of the township revolt I became an active supporter and began to make many contacts in the South African movement.

One of the outstanding figures of the township revolt was Moses Mayekiso, leader of the National Union of Metal Workers of South Africa (NUMSA) and a leading community activist in Alexandra township. As a shop steward in an engineering factory owned by the British Tyre and Rubber Company (BTR) I met Mayekiso when he came to Britain to gain support for the BTR Samcol strike in Natal. Not long after this Mayekiso was charged with conspiracy in relation to his activities in the Alexandra township revolt. In 1988 his union, NUMSA, sent to Britain his wife and a leading union activist, Bongani Mkhungo, to seek support in the workers' movement for the campaign for his release. I set about organising two public meetings for them in Manchester, where I was now living.

After a very well-attended public meeting the NUMSA member, Bongani Mkhungo, came back to my house to stay the night. But instead of sleeping we spent the whole night talking. We were each at a crossroads in the development of our own ideas, and as we talked our completely different experiences seemed to fit like pieces of a jigsaw, revealing a whole picture for the first time.

Bongani had spent his adult life building the trade union movement that had organised the workers' movement into such a powerful force that it was bringing apartheid rule to its knees. But now the unions' fight was suddenly being weakened by the rapid

INTRODUCTION 3

growth of a bureaucracy that was beginning to stifle the struggle. The fight against capitalism — a fight which union members had overwhelmingly supported — was being abandoned in favour of negotiations and a settlement with the white ruling class that would leave the latter's wealth and privilege largely untouched.

The Workers Revolutionary Party, of which I was a member, was one of the many parts of the fragmented Fourth International that had been founded by Trotsky and other Marxist opponents of Stalin in the Third (Communist) International. The WRP and its associated international movement had just been thrown into turmoil when its members revolted against the sect-like politics and methods into which the Fourth International had degenerated. This revolt was sparked off by the abuse of women members by the party leader, Gerry Healy. But this spark, which came shortly before the volcanic upsurge of working people all across eastern Europe, led some of us to try and understand how our 'anti-Stalinist' movement had ended up with many of the methods and policies of the Stalinists. So both Bongani and I had this common problem of bureaucratisation of our own organisations.

Bongani left the next morning, but he came back three weeks later. Instead of going back to South Africa he had been advised by his union to lie low in Britain for a while as the South African police were looking for him. He stayed for three months, working in the Transport and General Workers' Union office in Liverpool. At the weekends we would meet and carry on our discussions. This was the beginning of a friendship and political collaboration that have continued up to the present.

A few years after this first meeting I asked Bongani to write down the following account of his life.

Bob Myers
June 1997

THE STORY OF A SOUTH AFRICAN REVOLUTIONARY (1992)

How the struggle began

I was born in 1954. My family lived in a rural Zulu area. We lived in the traditional round mud houses with a bit of land — but not enough to live off. So my father had to go and live in the hostel and work in Durban. Sometimes he came home once a month. There was enough money to send us children to school. Many families couldn't afford that. We went to a mission school run by Catholic nuns. My favourite subject was history. They taught us how the settlers had come and brought civilisation to South Africa.

As a child I only went out of this country area on a few occasions. I didn't think about what was going on in South Africa. But there was one time when I saw something was wrong. About 1964 there was a poll tax. A woman doctor mobilised all the women of our area against that tax. The men had to go and pay the tax in the magistrates' court and the women marched on the roads, got on the buses and so on, to stop the men going to the court. Eventually the police came with Saracens (armoured vehicles) and took many of the women away, and the doctor went into exile. This was the first time I noticed the struggle — but I never really thought about these things until I started work.

In 1968 my father died. I was just about to start secondary school but this was not possible. There was no money. In the rural area there was no work. Now things were very hard. You had to have a work permit to work in the factories. You could only get the permit if you were living in the townships. Because my father had been ill for a year the rent on his place had not been paid and the government had repossessed it. So I had nowhere to live in town. In the end I got back my father's place in the township and was given a permit. At this time the police were very brutal. Everywhere they would stop people and check their permits. If your papers were not in order they would deport you back to the rural areas. To get the work permit you had to go to the office and show you were already a resident. Then there was a health check. They refused many people because they said black people carried many diseases.

All this was very strange to me as I had never been in town before. I went round the factories and, after a while, got a job. At this time there were no trade unions. The conditions in the factory were very bad. I worked there for one year and told them I was leaving because I could not live on the money. They said: 'Don't ever come back for a job here.' I told them I certainly wouldn't, because I knew how bad it was in there. After this I got a job at Dunlops, one of the biggest factories. Pay was much higher here and I was happy, but the men who were already there were dissatisfied because they had not had an increase for a long time. Also the general conditions were as harsh as at the place I had left. The white foremen called us 'boys'. To me that was not a good word for grown men.

In 1973 strikes broke out around Durban. The strikes were spontaneous. It was the bad conditions that caused the men to come out of the factories. I think the struggle started at the Coronation factory, where they made bricks. The workers there went on the rampage and demanded a wage increase. They went out in the street and marched, shouting Zulu war slogans. Then everyone started to join in. Even the people who didn't want to strike came out when they saw them marching past. In my factory there was a big man working on the mill. He saw the march and went round telling everyone they must down tools and join the strike. We went to the management and told them we wanted that money. They told us we must elect representatives to negotiate. We said: 'No, give us the money.'

Everywhere the police attacked the strikers, but the situation was beyond their control. Around Durban it had become a general strike. For a week it was chaos. People were coming into town, walking around the factories, and threatening the management. Then our management locked us out, but soon after agreed to give us what we wanted. We went back to work. The big man from the mill was sacked, though.

These strikes shook the country. The government set up a commission which recommended that the management should allow some unions to operate to help control the workers.

The rebirth of the unions

After the 1973 strike an old man in my factory started to tell me about this union: the Transport and General. I became interested. A few other people joined our discussions. Then we found out that the Metal and Allied Workers' Union (MAWU) was trying to organise in our industry, so four or five of us started going to their meetings. Even though, after the strike, some people in the ruling class wanted to allow unions, most employers were fighting to stop them. I don't think it was illegal to have a union, but any activity was suppressed.

Our meetings were clandestine and held at night. Our discussions were about how we were going to build the union.

I think these new unions were initiated by a few people who had come from the universities. Afterwards I found out that there had been the South African Congress of Trade Unions (SACTU), but this was led by people from the African National Congress (ANC), and I never came across it among the workers. From the start we said our unions must be independent from political parties. But mostly we concentrated on building the union. As the movement had started in our area we had to send people to other areas to organise the workers. In my factory we started to give out recruitment forms. We had to get 50 per cent of the workers before we could demand recognition. At first we just went to workers we could trust. Most people were not easy to convince. They didn't know anything about unions. They said: 'You just want to take our money.' We explained that if we were going to organise we needed money.

Our union targeted factories and sent people to give out leaflets outside factories early in the morning. One day my factory was targeted but, as often happened, the police came and arrested the activists. Then I heard groups of workers in our canteen discussing this and asking: 'What is this union that the management are so against?' Some said it was because the union activists were telling the truth. So I gave them recruitment forms. By now the workers knew I was a union organiser. One day the manager called me into his office and accused me of going round the factory organising the union. I told him I was doing all my work, so how could I be going round the factory? Two days later we got the 50 per cent and sent a letter asking for recognition. My name was put on as one of the representatives.

Now the management tried to make an agreement that would have made the union weak. We wouldn't agree to their terms. In 1984, at a lunch-time mass meeting, the workers decided to strike for recognition. We had to wait 30 days before the strike could be legal. Then we had a ballot. It was 100 per cent for strike action. We were now very confident. For the first day of the strike we stayed in the canteen. The next day we were all dismissed. So, in order to maintain our unity, we had to find a meeting-hall. We got a place and came together every day. A roll-call was taken, problems were discussed, and people were given different jobs to do. It was illegal to picket, but the management were trying to recruit new workers. So we formed a group called 'The Special Boys'. They went early each day to try and tell people why we were on strike. There were fights when people didn't listen. Of course, we had to work carefully to avoid the police. New workers were hired, because people were desperate for jobs. But management couldn't get production going as many of the jobs needed several months' training.

After three weeks the management called us back and agreed to recognition. This was a big victory. We marched through the streets, dancing and shouting. We jammed up the traffic, but the police couldn't touch us. They had to escort us. Workers from other factories came out to cheer us as we passed. When we went into the factory, management said people who had been involved in 'intimidation' at the gates were sacked. All the men refused to return to work. Then management backed down and we all went back to work. The foremen and some others who had scabbed were attacked and driven out of the factory. This went on for a week until the union organisers came and told the men to stop beating the foremen. So they were let back in, but they were never the same foremen again.

This was one of the first battles for recognition, and after we won that strike it was an example to other workers.

Living conditions in the township

At this time I was working a three-shift system. Early shift started at 6 a.m., but most of the townships are very far from the city, so I had to get up at 4 a.m. to get transport. I had to change twice on the way to the factory, first taking a taxi (minibus) and then trains. I got home from work after 6 p.m., sometimes much later if I was carrying out union duties. Everybody had to do this long journey. There was no work in the townships. There were a few shops, but they were very expensive, so most people had to go to town to shop as well. From where I was living, the journey took an hour — that's if you were lucky with transport. There was always a shortage of transport, so to get to work on time you had to leave very early because you never knew how long the journey will take. My township was started in the 1960s when a lot of squatters were kicked out of another township nearby. So people were given plots here on land owned by the KwaZulu government.

I had to buy materials and build my house. It was too small, but I had no alternative. I didn't have more money for materials. The house is about nine metres by four and has two rooms, one the kitchen and the other the bedroom. This is for eight of us: my wife and children and me. At least this house was made of blocks. A place I lived in before was made of mud bricks, and if it rained a lot the walls collapsed. The other problem when it rained was the roads.

Around the township there are just dirt roads, and of course in the rain they turn to mud. We had no services — no gas or electricity. We cooked on a Primus stove and used candles for lighting. The sanitation was the same bucket system that there was in the 1930s. You had a bucket in a row of outside toilets. Every day you had to put the bucket out for the sanitation truck. Often it didn't come. Maybe there was a strike or something like that. Then the buckets sat outside all day, which was very unhealthy. The biggest problem was water. There was a pipe outside about 30 metres away, so you had to do a lot of fetching water. I made a shelter outside my house where we could have a bath. There was a lot of discontent over conditions in the township, but there was no one organising any kind of action to improve things.

The children could go to school, but it was very bad. There were too many children. Maybe 10,000 people lived in this township, but there were only a couple of primary schools and one high school. Many classes had more than 50 children. Also there were clashes between people from the rural areas and those living in the township. The school was under the control of the KwaZulu government and people from the rural areas said it should be for their children. Mostly the children just played around outside the house. There were no medical facilities in the township, so if any of them were sick you had to travel to town. Of course you had to pay for any medical treatment. The only recreation facilities were football pitches that the young men made for themselves. But the workers were just going to work and coming home to eat and sleep. All the people there were workers so there was not much problem with crime, unlike some of the townships where there was high unemployment. Of course, once the violence started everything changed.

Conditions in the township were bad enough, but many people were in even worse conditions, especially those living in the hostels. These are the big compounds with thousands of people living in them. Four or five people share a small room and a tiny kitchen. They have to keep all their belongings and their food and plates under their beds. There are communal washrooms and toilets. The hostels were built to accommodate migrant workers, who had to leave families far away and come to work in the factories. Many workers have no alternative but to live in these places. The hostels are only for men. But of course there are women in the hostels, and this causes lots of fights and problems. There is no privacy, so a man who has a girl-friend has to bring her to the room he shares with the other men. There are some rooms the married men can book if their wives come to see them, but the wife can stay for only two weeks and then she must go back to the Homeland. All of these things made us realise that in the trade unions we must focus on bad housing, high rents, and things like that.

From union to community organisation

The year 1984 was the year of the youth uprising. Unions in the Federation of South African Trade Unions (FOSATU) were still independent of any political party. But now the United Democratic Front (UDF) had been formed during the campaign to boycott Prime Minister P.W. Botha's attempt to set up a tripartite government including the Indian and 'Coloured' communities. I was involved in the UDF committee organising a consumer boycott of white-owned shops in our area. The workers were very active in this campaign. We discussed it inside the factories.

In 1984 violence began in the townships. First a woman from the boycott campaign was killed. Inkatha (the Zulu political organisation formed in 1975 by Chief Gatsha Buthelezi) was not very active then but it opposed the boycott. The youth blamed Inkatha for her death and went on the rampage, attacking town councillors who belonged to Inkatha as well as shops and government offices, most of which were staffed by Inkatha supporters. To defend themselves these people began to mobilise behind the Inkatha war-lords in collusion with the police. We had big problems. There were some workers who supported Inkatha. They were told not to follow the calls the youth were making. Sometimes they forced their way to work during a stayaway the youth had called. Then there were clashes. During that time Inkatha and the police killed many workers. The UDF made no real attempt

THE STORY OF A SOUTH AFRICAN REVOLUTIONARY 11

to defend the workers against the Inkatha war-lords. In fact most UDF leaders went underground after some of them were arrested. In this tense situation the unions had to intervene. The shop stewards called a meeting with the youth, not to stop their actions but to bring some discipline to the situation. We set up joint committees with the youth and began to work well together. We argued for socialism and the youth were very enthusiastic about this, but some of the UDF leaders were strongly opposed.

The situation in the factories was very tense. Often many people could not get to work because of the fighting. The youth's actions drove some workers towards Inkatha. For instance, early on the youth had 'necklaced' [put a burning tyre round the neck of] a worker from one of the hostels who had tried to go to work. Inkatha war-lords called a meeting in the area and promised to protect people from the youth. So the problem was that some workers were siding with Inkatha and the police against the youth.

We had meetings inside the factories to try and discourage our members from joining Inkatha. In our factory, with our strong union, we were able to persuade most people not to join, but it was difficult.

Elsewhere people did join. They did not see why they should support the youth. Besides, a lot of criminal elements used the youth's actions as a cover. So there were a lot of antagonisms.

At this time no one had any idea where these struggles were leading. It was a spontaneous outburst. Everybody was just going from day to day, without planning, meetings, or leadership. The UDF simply tried to ride on the youth's militancy. The UDF slogan was: 'Make the townships ungovernable.' The youth liked this slogan and were attacking all the local representatives of government. Several years later we found out that while the ANC was encouraging this it was already conducting secret negotiations with the top level of the ruling class. The struggle died down under the repression of the police and the efforts of the UDF and the Church to discourage people.

Only the unions carried on their activities. But now we had experience of trying to organise the community. We had tried to organise township committees. The problem was that the UDF came to every meeting just to tell the workers what to do. This discouraged people.

This was repeated after Nelson Mandela's release in February 1990. Again the youth were fighting with the police. Many people were being killed. The UDF didn't know what to do. I proposed that we should call a general meeting of the township. Ten thousand people came to it. I felt that the UDF speeches were just window-dressing. They weren't going to do anything.

I called for discipline among the youth and said they must stop 'necklacing' anybody they felt like killing. I said we needed a defence committee to unite the workers with the youth. So I organised a workshop for some of the leading people, to discuss how we were going to form our structures. None of the UDF people came. I explained how we should organise at every level, with accountability of committees. We wanted to stop people just acting on their own. The youth were pleased about this organisation. We divided the township into areas and started to organise. It was very effective. UDF leaders came to the township and said that this structure was very wrong, because nothing was under the UDF's control. They managed to break it all up.

Funerals

One year our union held its general meeting near Durban. It was not only union members who attended the rally in the stadium. Lots of youth came too. Because of what the unions had done in 1984 the youth gave great support to the workers' activities. They would come with banners and shout for socialism, even though most of them were UDF supporters. I was one of the marshals trying to get everyone into the rally without trouble. Already in the morning we had a confrontation with the police, who tried to stop people singing as they marched into the stadium. We had the rally — then, as people were leaving, the police opened fire. I saw one of our stewards hit. We carried him away. Everyone was running to get away.

The next morning I was called from work to the mortuary to

identify bodies. I didn't recognise anyone. But I was given names, and back at work someone knew that one of those names was a young man who had been at our rally. So our shop stewards met. We said we must do something because this young man was killed attending our rally. We went to see his family and told them that the workers wanted to arrange the funeral. They agreed. We returned to the factory and collected money.

As we were going back to the family we met a man from the UDF. He said they must arrange the funeral as the young man was their member. We told him: 'No. That youth was killed participating with the workers.' We went to the family and they agreed with us. So we organised the funeral. Many of the workers came and I gave the funeral speech. I talked about the struggle of the working class for socialism.

One May Day, as usual, we were celebrating the international struggle. Everywhere workers were taking strike action to attend a rally in a stadium. That year however Inkatha was also holding a rally nearby to launch its so-called 'Union'. But no workers from the factories were going to the Inkatha rally. Inkatha had to bring all the people by train and bus from the rural areas. Later the press printed letters showing that the police paid for Inkatha's stadium and transport. All the workers went to our rally. After the rally some of the people were waiting at a station when a train carrying people from the Inkatha rally pulled in. One of the war-lords started shooting, and a young man was killed.

The next morning, when we heard about this, our stewards' committee met. Again the shop stewards went to see the family. At first his mother was saying that it was her son's fault. If he had stayed at home he would not be dead.

We explained: 'No. It is the struggle of the working class. Tomorrow the youth will be workers. They must participate in these activities.' So she agreed, and it was decided that we would make all the arrangements for the funeral.

But now our union officials were not enthusiastic about helping.

They said it was not union business. So we did everything through the stewards. We collected money from the workers and arranged that funeral. Many people attended.

In our factory I worked with a quiet young man. One day we were talking about the people being killed by the police. He said to me: 'If they come for me I am taking one of them with me to the grave.' I thought he was joking. Later we were on strike. First thing in the morning a worker came to our strike meeting and said that this young man had been killed. We went to his house. It was deserted. Everything was smashed to pieces and full of bullet-holes.

None of the neighbours would tell us what had happened. Later we found where my workmate's family had fled to. They told us that he had had two visitors. Then the police had telephoned to tell them that the house was surrounded and they must all give themselves up. The young man and his visitors made the family leave the house while they themselves stayed behind. Then shooting started. The gun battle went on for five hours. The three men were killed, as were several police. Now we understood that they must have been members of Umkhonto we Sizwe (MK, the ANC military unit). Because of that everyone was scared to have anything to do with the funeral. They thought the police would be after them too. But for us this was one of our union members. The UDF and the union officials didn't want to help with the funeral, so again we organised it. But now even many people in our factory were scared to attend.

When we got to the cemetery we found many police stopping us. Two helicopters were flying overhead. The police told us that no woman could go into the cemetery and that we had only five minutes to bury that man. There must be no singing. We were very scared. When we started to bury him we were surrounded by police with guns pointing at us. I went to the police commander and told him that it was impossible to bury someone in five minutes. We buried that man in silence.

He had died as he said — but it was the workers and some youth who buried him, not his own organisation.

The ANC strangles the unions

After the 1984 township revolt was crushed the only activity was in the unions. In the rubber industry, the management's intransigence made us set about forming a shop stewards' combined committee to unite all the factories. The 1984 events had convinced us even more of the need for socialism. Joe Foster, one of the founders of FOSATU, had talked about the need to build a workers' party, but we still thought that the unions would get us to socialism. I organised classes for our union shop stewards in the region. These meetings went from 7 p.m. Saturday to 7 a.m. Sunday, with short breaks for refreshments. Because of our problems this was the only time it was possible to get everyone together.

We discussed socialism. Speakers were invited to tell us about things like the Russian revolution. We had no books at all, so we could only talk. The workers discussed the ANC's 'Freedom Charter' and we saw it was just minimum demands. It had no interest for us. We were interested in what had happened in Russia, because we thought there was socialism there. Questions were raised about things like Solidarność in Poland, but all we could understand was that there was a lack of democracy in the socialist countries because of the 'command economy'. The stewards would report back these discussions to their workers. That was the way we always worked. Although we had these discussions we didn't get a clear picture of what was to be done. All we got from our speakers was history lessons. At that time some ANC supporters were talking with us, trying to convince us that the 'two-stage theory' was right. (This was the policy of the South African Communist Party, which said that the first stage of the story was a democratic black capitalist government which would create the conditions for workers to fight for socialism.) As workers we said: 'No, we can't have that. Once you reach the first stage you never come to the second stage.' These people had no influence inside FOSATU. I was a delegate to our union's first national conference, where everyone voted for socialism.

The exiled ANC was very influential in the UDF. It was trying to influence FOSATU, but couldn't do so. So it started looking for other means to control FOSATU. There were unions outside FOSATU. The biggest was the National Union of Miners (NUM), but there were many small ones too. Years earlier the ANC had formed the South African Congress of Trade Unions, but it had very few members, only organisers. The UDF had influence over these organisations. Of course, we all wanted a single union federation, especially with the NUM in it. My union started talks with those little UDF unions in our industry. Their leaders saw that their unions were crumbling. Everyone was joining the FOSATU unions. So, before they vanished completely, they moved in to propose mergers. So their leaders got influence in our union. Now there was a proposed merger of all the unions. This was done with the formation of the Confederation of South African Trade Unions (COSATU). When we formed our merged union we were urged to adopt the ANC's 'Freedom Charter'. People from the UDF came to our conference to tell us it was impossible to go straight to socialism and that the only way to get our freedom was through the ANC. The workers didn't agree with this. The UDF people were shouting at the workers, but still they wouldn't adopt the 'Freedom Charter'.

In 1987 we took our 'Workers' Charter' to the congress of the new federation, COSATU. There was a big battle. Now there was something new in our unions. The leadership saw it could not get agreement with the workers on this issue, so they just appointed some committees to investigate and decide. Finally the union leaders adopted the 'Freedom Charter' but without ever going to the members. It wasn't the workers who adopted the 'Freedom Charter'. This was the first time that things had not been democratically taken to the workers. Though the workers didn't agree with the Charter they didn't want to criticise the leaders because they felt that would split the unions.

Looking back, I can see that in 1984 the ANC started having secret talks with the ruling class — with the Anglo-American Corporation, the biggest company in South Africa. Both sides in these talks were afraid of socialism. The only way to fulfil their aims was to take away the democracy within the unions so that the workers could not question what was going on in the negotiations.

So, in the same way as the 'Freedom Charter' was adopted, now an alliance of the unions, the South African Communist Party (SACP) and the ANC was agreed without any reference to the shop floor. We were just told that they were in an alliance. More and more decisions were reported back as having already been taken. In the past the workers were always consulted. Now union democracy was vanishing.

From the unions to the revolutionary party

The 1973 spontaneous strike taught many of us the need for unity among the workers to protect us against the employers. This unity could only be achieved through the unions. The growth of the unions was rapid and led to many strikes for recognition and better conditions. The employers responded brutally. Again and again police were used to try and crush the strikes. Shop stewards were murdered. But we managed to win many things, and we also became conscious of ourselves as a class. It became clear to me, and to many other workers, that we could only be free when we got rid of the capitalist class and nationalised the industries. We saw the wealth we created and we saw it stolen from us. The problem was how to stop this robbery. We knew we could not do without our unions, but we also saw that this political problem had to be discussed. This discussion went on in different ways in different places. I organised the night-time workshops in our area to discuss things like the Russian revolution. Many of us became clear we were for socialism — but we remained very confused about what was to be done.

The leaders of the exiled movements — the ANC and SACP — were very clear about what their supporters in the country should be doing. They were pushing their programme, the 'Freedom Charter'. They had to present it as a socialist charter to try and get the workers' support. But there were many of us who had learnt enough to know that this 'Freedom Charter' was not a programme for socialism. Above all, workers had seen the *actions* of people who supported the Charter. All these people had ever done was undermine our fighting unity. The SACP supporters put forward many arguments to justify the 'Freedom Charter' as being a first stage towards socialism. They said it was impossible just to sweep capitalism away. First we must fight for a capitalism with majority rule. I didn't agree with this. In fact we can see today that these same people can't even fight seriously for majority rule. But those of us who opposed them couldn't see how to go forward.

Our big problem was that we didn't understand the real nature of the Stalinists in the SACP. Remember that there were no books available to us. We knew nothing of the history of Stalinism, nothing about the millions of workers around the world whom it had suppressed. We were confused, whereas they were organised. Slowly they brought our movement under their control. As we saw it, there were two different routes to socialism, and we disagreed with their route.

During this time some people went abroad on the union's behalf. I went to Britain with the wife of our union President Moses Mayekiso, who was under arrest, charged with conspiracy — we went to speak at solidarity rallies.

I learnt many interesting things there about the long struggle there had been against Stalin and the policies of the Communist Parties. But most of these groups were supporting the ANC or telling us that we had to revolutionise it. From my point of view this was not possible. So I still saw no way forward. By this time I was unemployed as I had been sacked for going to a union conference in Zimbabwe on behalf of my union. So I worked full time for the union. Then I met some people who were fighting to rebuild the Fourth International. They were trying to organise an international conference with the purpose of rebuilding an international workers' movement to bring together revolutionary workers from every country in the world. From this discussion we learnt about the history of the Fourth International that had been founded by the members of the Communist Parties who had fought against Stalin and his policy of 'socialism in one country' and the two-stage theory. We also now began to understand why so many socialist groups that were against Stalinism still supported the ANC. The Fourth International had also moved away from its struggle to unite the workers and instead followed behind the reformist and Stalinist parties. Some of the people we were talking to were members of the Workers Revolutionary Party in Britain who had just kicked out their own leaders because of this and had begun to try and rebuild their movement on real socialist principles.

I and another comrade from Dunlops went to that international conference in Budapest in 1990. We went back to South Africa and told our comrades that the only way to continue our fight for socialism was to help rebuild the Fourth International, because it was founded to continue the struggle of Marx and Lenin — the struggle to unite the workers of the world into a party that could enable the workers to emancipate themselves. To me in South Africa this was a big change. At last we understood. There were not two routes to socialism, but only this fight to build the International. Those who proposed the 'Freedom Charter' wanted only to sabotage the workers' fight for socialism.

Even though there was only a small group of us discussing these new ideas we knew what we had to do. We began to build a section of the Fourth International among the workers and youth of South Africa.

Lies and rumours

One of the people who had gone to the conference of the Fourth International in Budapest was a shop steward in Dunlops. Because of the direction the union leaders were now taking it was impossible for him to go to Budapest representing the union. He just went as an individual. Some of the shop stewards, who now supported the 'Freedom Charter', found out he had gone. On his return they started to ask why he had gone. Who had paid his fares? Who gave him a mandate to go? Some of the stewards started spreading rumours among the workers. They told them that he had gone abroad without permission, that he had been paid by the South African government, that thousands of rand had been made available to him to disrupt COSATU, and so on.

They reported all these things to a mass meeting without any proper consultation with the two comrades who had gone to

Budapest. They wanted the workers to remove this man. To say that he had been paid by the government was really to call on the workers to kill him, because that was what was happening to spies at that time. The workers knew that in the past anyone who went anywhere had to get permission from the union and had to report back. That was our democracy. What they didn't see so clearly was that the union leaders themselves had begun acting behind everyone's back.

So now our comrade got up in front of the workers and explained why he went. That he had to know about the struggle for socialism. That he had gone as an individual because the union no longer fought for socialism. That workers in Britain paid his fares. Then the workers asked the other stewards: 'What is wrong with this man going to learn about socialism? That is what we have been calling for all this time. This is what we have been singing about for years.' The shop stewards couldn't answer that. Then they started organising in our comrade's section in the factory, trying to get the men to deselect their steward. They succeeded in making the men call a section meeting. Again he explained why he had gone to Budapest. He explained about socialism, about all the things he had learnt at the conference. The workers supported him.

The same lies were being spread through the union outside the factory. A meeting of the local committee was called where all the shop stewards from different factories were present. The same accusations were put now to both. We explained that they wanted to form an independent workers' party. So then people said: 'Why do you want to form a party when we have COSATU and the ANC and the SACP?' We replied that we had no problem with COSATU. It was the union but it was not a political party. We were against the ANC because it was not a workers' party and we were against the SACP because it was totally subordinated to the ANC. Then people in the local turned on these shop stewards who had spread the rumours and told them that they had been distorting things and must go back to the factory and tell the workers the truth.

All this was taking place just when the government had made the ANC and the SACP legal. Many workers were worried that the alliance of the unions with these two organisations was never discussed by the workers. Union officials had suddenly become recruiting officers for the ANC and SACP, coming into the factories with recruitment forms. But in the big factories the workers were against that. They asked: 'Why must we join the ANC, the SACP? When we were fighting for our unions these organisations were nowhere.' They had known for a long time that the ANC was not a workers' movement, and they couldn't distinguish the SACP from the ANC. People saw them as the same thing.

One day I met a man I used to work with. He told me that he had gone with four friends to the SACP's launch rally. That was a twelve-hour return journey for them. He wanted a workers' party. At the rally the SACP gave out recruitment forms. But two months later he still hadn't filled his in. All this gave us new contacts.

The rumours about our visit to Budapest spread many miles. People who knew me rang me up to check these stories. Then I could tell them the truth and invite them to our discussions. A few came, but most still followed the union leaders. But sometimes, even months after talking, people come to contact us because now they see we were right. So, even though it was very difficult for us to organise with no money and with all the union officials against us, we began to get people to our discussion forums who wanted to find out about our ideas of an independent workers' party in South Africa.

ANC unbanned

Our township was under the control of the KwaZulu government of Gatsha Buthelezi but no one was a member of Inkatha. They were all workers. After the unbanning of the ANC people were very enthusiastic. They thought this was going to bring them their liberation. The day Mandela was released there were big rallies all over the country. The youth and the workers were marching and dancing in the streets. Others were watching events on the television. Inkatha was against that. Buthelezi, the Inkatha leader, saw his influence would vanish. The government had given him the territory of KwaZulu to rule. South Africa under ANC rule would do away with his 'country'. So the KwaZulu police provoked clashes with the youth and started to shoot.

I tried to contact the lawyers as the police had gone on the rampage. Then the youth leaders came to my house. Even as we started to discuss what to do we had to flee because the KwaZulu police were coming and shooting all over the place. When I returned I found that the youth had burnt down my neighbour's house. They suspected he was an Inkatha supporter. Maybe he was. I don't know. We had had violence since 1985, but what developed in the next few weeks was chaos. Even different groups of taxi-drivers were killing each other. My cousin was killed in the crossfire of one of their battles. The youth were fleeing from the townships because they were Inkatha's main target. Houses were being burnt. People were being killed. Everyone was frightened. Especially at night you could hear the gunfire and know people were dying. The school system collapsed. The children were afraid to go to school. My five-year-old son ran under the bed every time he heard the shooting.

While all these people were being killed the ANC organised a welcome rally in the area for Mandela. This was the biggest rally we had ever seen. People were excited to see Mandela. But the applause turned to disappointment. Mandela praised Buthelezi and said he wanted to meet him. Then he called on the people to throw their weapons in the sea. But people asked: 'How are we to defend ourselves from the police and Inkatha vigilantes?' I was surprised to see that old man who had spent many years in jail being heckled at his first rally. But it was very risky for people even to come to this rally. They didn't know what would happen to them when they went home. The rally marshals had helped the police to disarm everyone who went into that rally. Afterwards Inkatha ambushed some people leaving the rally and ten people were killed. So how could Mandela call on us to throw our weapons away?

Some of us tried to organise the defence of the township. But the UDF undermined our efforts because the structures we tried to create were not under their control. Also the violence made it difficult to organise. Our political discussion group could hardly meet. It was the same for the union. Everyone had to rush home from work before dark. If you were on the night-shift you had to go to work in the afternoon to avoid being on the road in the dark. And it was difficult for people to be at meetings because they wanted to be at home to protect their families. This violence was not just from Inkatha and the police, however. When the ANC was unbanned the youth started to organise a branch in the township. At first their branch grew, but not many workers joined, and when a lot of young people became disillusioned with the ANC it all fell apart. The ANC youth leaders now started to harass people who did not support their organisation. It was the same in other townships. There were many incidents in which the ANC killed people from rival organisations. In some townships the youth even began to organise groups to defend themselves against the activities of the so-called 'ANC People's Committees'.

My family and I had to flee from our home because of harassment from the ANC. They came with guns and threatened my children and told them they would return and kill me. Even though we knew it was the ruling class that was behind all the killings, the ANC and South African CP bore a heavy responsibility for the violence. In 1984 they were encouraging the youth to necklace and kill anyone they didn't agree with. Winnie Mandela in particular encouraged the youth in this way and used them to get rid of her enemies. So now the ANC and South African CP were telling their supporters that it was OK to kill anyone who was not supporting the ANC. In the past, in the unions, we could have democratic discussion. But now in the townships arguments were being settled with guns. This played into the hand of the provocateurs arranged by the government. After the ANC was unbanned thousands of people were killed. In Natal it came close to civil war.

What happened in the liberation armies
We had seen the way the ANC encouraged its supporters to suppress their political opponents. Soon we also learnt that this suppression had gone on for a long time in the so-called 'liberation' armies.

On the border of South Africa is Namibia, where people have long been fighting against foreign rule, first by Germany, then by South Africa. In South Africa many people followed the Namibians' struggle for independence, which was opposed by the South African regime until finally the imperialists in the United Nations struck a deal between the South African regime and the leaders of the South West Africa People's Organisation (SWAPO), a Namibian liberation movement. The South African trade unions rallied the workers behind SWAPO. They issued pamphlets and took collections in the factories to help SWAPO in the independence elections. Many South African workers were enthusiastic about this election in Namibia. But some of us had no trust in SWAPO. As soon as the elections under UN supervision were agreed the SWAPO leaders told their armed fighters outside the country to return. How could SWAPO have such trust in the UN and the South African regime? As the fighters crossed the border the South African army murdered many of them while the UN stood watching. They were sent into a trap.

Liberation fighters were killed in other ways. We had heard on the radio in South Africa that there had been people in the People's Liberation Army of Namibia (PLAN, the SWAPO armed wing) who had been imprisoned, tortured or killed by their own organisation. As the South African regime was putting out this news to try and discredit SWAPO we didn't bother to listen. However, I went to Namibia before the elections and there I met with SWAPO members whom SWAPO security forces had kept in pits in the ground for many years. They had accused them of being spies. After listening to all sides it was clear that most of them were loyal SWAPO members and that they had been imprisoned because SWAPO was a very undemocratic organisation and also had security men trained in east Germany and Romania.

The people I met told me that the SWAPO leaders were against the youth because the youth had been fighting for democracy in the organisation and also because they were for socialism. Now the press in South Africa also began to publish the same sort of story about MK, the ANC's armed wing. Again most people dismissed this as government propaganda, but because of what I had learnt in Namibia I got in touch with a group of MK soldiers in Kenya who had written an account of mutinies inside MK over the lack of democracy.

Our discussion group managed to invite two MK soldiers who had been involved in the mutinies to come to a meeting. They told us of terrible things that had happened to many young fighters at the hands of ANC security forces. Now the workers at the meeting really began to see the full picture. Of course we already disagreed with the ANC but now, with the experiences in the unions and in MK, we saw that the South African CP would really use every means to stop the working class from overthrowing capitalism.

So we circulated the articles the MK people had written. Of course this was not easy. A lot of people only saw this as attacking the ANC, which they supported. They saw it as helping the regime. But we carried on because we knew that the working class could not liberate itself with leaders of this kind, who stifle all discussion and do not allow any criticism.

These MK fighters had been the militant youth of the townships in 1984. They had gone abroad for military training because they had seen that stones would not bring down the regime. But when they got to the ANC camps in Angola and elsewhere they were really in a trap. They were never allowed to go back and fight.

Now, with the beginning of negotiations between the ANC and F.W. de Klerk, many of them were returning to the country. Those who remained loyal to the ANC were given money and jobs, but those who had criticised the movement and who returned by themselves got no help. They were returning without money or jobs. All they had was their disillusion with the ANC. They wanted to form an association to protect themselves and publicise what had happened to them. If the socialist workers could have helped these people to do this, and could have helped them to understand what had happened to them, it would have been a big step forward for us. But we had no resources. Even the MK people from Kenya were all split up far apart in different parts of South Africa after their return. They didn't even have money to write to each other. Soon right-wing forces who had money were able to use, for their own purposes, the returnees' disillusion and their fear for their lives, and were able to win some of them, for the moment, to an organisation that the state financed to attack the ANC. But not all of them were deceived like that. Some of them were able to understand what had happened to them, and have joined us in the fight for socialism.

Just as in Namibia, these atrocities inside the liberation movement came to be very widely talked about. For the moment most workers don't understand what went on. But this fraud of 'armed struggle' must become known to every worker. There was no armed struggle. And the leaders who organised the beatings, torture and murders of some of our best young people will, with state forces under their control, do the same things to workers who challenge them. I know many people think we were wrong to publicise the stories about the mutinies. They thought we were undermining the struggle because the regime was telling the same stories. But we believe that the workers must stand by the youth who went to fight for socialism and were suppressed by ANC 'security forces'.

Two SWAPO women in Namibia told me that when SWAPO security arrested them they were taken to a place where they were beaten and tortured. That place was called a 'Marxist Education Centre'. Inside our country, in the unions, these leaders tried to use their so-called 'Marxism' to silence people. It is not possible to be in favour of socialism and then be quiet about these things.

Whose liberation are we fighting for?

After white rule ended in Zimbabwe I went to a trade union conference in Harare. A Zimbabwe trade unionist told me that when the workers had been fighting the liberation war against the Smith regime they hadn't realised that they were fighting alongside their future oppressors — the black capitalists in Robert Mugabe's government. He told me that the South African workers must not make the same mistake as they had, especially since the workers in Zimbabwe placed so much of their hopes on the workers in South Africa. At that time I don't think many South Africans would have understood his warning. But today the leaders of the ANC and the

South African CP are in an alliance with the bosses, and the union leaders are supporting this alliance — with the same people who have treated generations of workers so badly. The warning from Zimbabwe was right. These 'liberation' leaders are the enemies of the workers. These leaders have always tried to make sure that the voice of the Zimbabwe working class was not heard in South Africa. The capitalists in the 'liberation movements' and their Moscow allies only shouted about Mugabe's victory, or about Nujoma in Namibia, not about how the workers still faced oppression. I have also now found out that most of the socialist groups around the world were also too busy celebrating Mugabe's victory to hear the voice of the workers.

All around the world the workers' voice was very weak. Stalinists, nationalists, bureaucrats and reformists were all shouting loudly that they represented the workers while in fact they silenced them. Many people who said they were revolutionaries got confused about who they were listening to and ended up helping to silence the workers. So we in South Africa have had the problem that we have had to learn many things from our own experiences even though other workers, elsewhere in the world, had already been through similar problems and could have helped us with many things. Everywhere the workers have been kept isolated from each other.

In South Africa we know we cannot just fight against the bosses there. In every city you will see names like Toyota, BTR, Mercedes and so on. There is not a country in the world that does not have people who have grown rich from our suffering. We know we are going to have to fight all of them. We also know that the working class does not stop at the borders of South Africa. These borders were drawn on maps by the English anyway. There are workers in Angola who suffered years of civil war organised by South Africa. Look at what happened in Somalia, where people died like ants from starvation while there was so much food in Europe. The US went in. But they didn't go to help the workers and peasants. The US and its banks caused the starvation in the first place. They went in to make sure capitalism was kept safe.

So we know we must build an international workers' party.

Everywhere the unions are being hijacked by the bureaucrats on behalf of the capitalists. As workers, we must come together around the world to take back our unions. We must stop these bureaucrats keeping the workers of one country separate from those of another. In South Africa in my lifetime the unions have grown up and become very strong — and then they have been taken out of the control of the workers who built them.

We in the Workers International are fighting to organise the working class so that it can rid itself of these people. The ANC, the South African CP and the union leaders may be able to have an alliance with the bosses. But the workers know that there can never be an alliance between them and the bosses. We know we must build this revolutionary party. At the moment we have some big problems. We are only a few people. We have no money, no office, no equipment. Sometimes, for weeks on end, it is difficult for us to contact each other. But the one thing we have got from being part of the Workers International is an understanding of what needs to be done. We know who our friends are — and our enemies. Now we are able to begin a campaign in the unions and among the youth to oppose the Unity Government. The problems are very great at times, but we will not give up.

The South African CP used to try and fool the workers that it was a party like Lenin's. They tried to fool the workers that it would be a step towards socialism if we got the ANC in government. Now their masters in eastern Europe have stopped pretending to be socialists. They are all trying to become capitalists as fast as they can. In South Africa it was Joe Slovo, a leader of the South African CP, who proposed that the ANC should join the de Klerk government. Soon workers who go on strike or protest at unemployment or bad housing will be facing the police or the army commanded by a government with the ANC in it.

We have to bring together every worker and youth who is going to lead the fight for the workers against such a government. We have to bring them together into the Fourth International which was founded by the socialists whom Stalin could not silence in the 1930s, who fought to keep alive working-class internationalism and working-class principles. I hope that one day I can meet that comrade from Zimbabwe again. We should be in the same party, organising our campaign against the bosses just as they plan to defeat the workers internationally. We have to unite workers in every country to fight for our class against this terrible system of capitalism which is making so many people suffer, above all here in Africa.

FIGHTING CORRUPTION

When Bongani and I first met he and other South African trade unionists were trying to get to grips with the rapid bureaucratisation of their unions. They had two aims: to retain the previous democracy so far as possible, and to try and understand what was happening. But it was not just trade unionists who were dealing with this problem. Not long after meeting Bongani I helped organise another speaking tour in Britain, this time for Ndamona and Panduleni Kali, twin sisters from Namibia.

Following the 1985 revolt in the Workers Revolutionary Party in Britain, we had begun to make contacts with revolutionaries around the world to try and understand what had happened inside our movement. These international discussions coalesced into a 'preparatory committee' which eventually organised the conference in Budapest that Bongani refers to in his life story. Taking part in this committee prior to the conference were representatives from a South African group, the Workers International League of South Africa (WILSA). Though they did not tell us, their group had members in Namibia. But the South African and Namibian members were in a growing conflict. Namibia had just won its independence from South African apartheid rule. The Namibian members wanted to campaign publicly on an issue that was rocking the country — the fate of hundreds of liberation fighters in SWAPO (South West Africa People's Organisation) who had been imprisoned, tortured

FIGHTING CORRUPTION

and even murdered by their own organisation. The South African WILSA members were against them raising this issue. They wanted to concentrate all their efforts on getting SWAPO elected. They said that to raise this issue of the missing fighters would discredit SWAPO and help the various reactionary parties contesting the election.

The first we knew about this in Britain was when the Namibian members, who assumed that the 'preparatory committee' knew all about the dispute, sent a telegram announcing that they were launching their own open party in Namibia and would make the fate of the 'missing liberation fighters their main election issue.

With our own recent experience of a fight against a corrupt leadership we took no time in sending the Namibians our support. WILSA then departed from the 'preparatory committee' and soon after joined the African National Congress.

Not long after this we organised for Ndamona and Panduleni, two of the people who had been imprisoned and tortured by SWAPO, to come to Britain. The next chapter is what they told us.

Bob Myers
June 1997

HOW SWAPO TORTURED ITS OWN FIGHTERS (1989)

THIS, largely in their own words, is the story of what happened to Ndamona and Panduleni Kali, two former SWAPO liberation fighters, when, with hundreds of others, they were detained and tortured by the leaders of their own organisation. Ndamona and Panduleni, who are twin sisters, came to Britain to expose the scandal of SWAPO's internal terror.

They joined SWAPO in 1974 at the age of 15. They left Namibia in 1978, were given military training in 1979 at the Tobias Hainyeko Training Centre in Angola, and were then sent to the Soviet Union (Ndamona) and Cuba (Panduleni). In 1980 Ndamona joined her sister in Cuba, where both entered the university in the following year. They were recalled to Angola before they could take their degrees.

On 8 November 1984 we were called by the man responsible for foreign students, who told us we had to go and sign some SWAPO papers. A Cuban woman, who we later heard was State Security, ordered us to undress, without any explanation. She put on some gloves and examined us internally. We were ordered to put on our clothes again, and told that one of us had to go under escort to our hostel room and separate our things from the university property. All this time we were asking why this was happening.

HOW SWAPO TORTURED ITS OWN FIGHTERS 33

Ndamona, who went to the hostel, found to her surprise that most of their belongings were already packed. She was asked to hand over the keys.

They drove us to the Ministry of State Security in the province of Camaquey, then handcuffed us and took us to Havana, a journey lasting ten hours. At Havana we were again told to undress. They carried out another internal examination and we were put in a cell, where we stayed for four days.

On the second day we demanded to see the chief official there. We said we needed an explanation because we were certain that we had never committed any crime on Cuban soil. It did not enter our heads that SWAPO had any hand in this. We even demanded to see our SWAPO representative so that we could tell him about all these things the Cuban government was doing to us.

Panduleni: I was taken before two men, one black and one white. The white man I later knew was a Cuban and the black one a Namibian. The Namibian told me he was sent by SWAPO to tell us that we are needed in Africa. He said there was a small problem we had to solve in Africa and then after solving it we would come back and continue our studies.

When Panduleni was taken back to the cell Ndamona was ordered out to the room with the two men and she went through the same procedures.

Ndamona: This part of the whole experience, which lasted five years, is very vivid because it was such a shock to be one minute living the life of a student in what we thought was a socialist country, happy, studying, with friends — and the next minute to be taken by armed security forces, locked up, strip-searched, handcuffed and transported miles away to a cell, with all our belongings packed by armed security guards.

On the fifth day we were escorted to the military airport.

Then something which later became a way of life manifested

itself: asking for permission to visit the toilet. This order was made by the Cuban state security forces. At mealtimes the stewardess was ordered to remove the plastic knives. We were different from all other passengers, and this was obvious for all to see.

When we landed in Luanda we were again handed over to the Cuban Security Forces. When the SWAPO truck came they handed us over to SWAPO. We were taken to a post in the bush where we stayed for a week. We were guarded by people who were made responsible for giving us our food and water, and we had to ask these people if we wanted to go to the toilet, and they accompanied us there. We later learned that these people had come from the Soviet Union and were SWAPO Security. We were told to pack our belongings because we were to proceed to Lubango.

When we entered the trucks, we found two male comrades of ours already in the truck with their hands tied behind their backs. They were seated and covered with a blanket. One of them was screaming with pain because his hands were tied very tightly and he was begging them to loosen them, but the only response was cynical laughter. On the journey, which lasted more than two days, the male comrades' hands were untied, but they were never allowed to sleep without their hands being tied behind their backs, and therefore they could hardly sleep. At Lubango we were separated from the male comrades, and we did not see them again for five years.

The next morning we were asked to write our autobiographies. After that the two of us were separated and we did not see each other again for two years.

Panduleni: After I wrote my autobiography, I was told to go in a small room and I slept on the floor with only one blanket. About two o'clock in the morning I was called out. I went to the office, where I found six men, with a small lantern. They asked me to repeat my autobiography — speak it — which I did.

They then told me that it was high time that I started to be serious: 'SWAPO knows everything about you — your whole activities inside and outside Namibia. Don't think that anything you have done is a secret.' They asked me if I was ready to talk peacefully or was I ready for violence. I said I had told them the truth and if they went to violence that was up to them.

They stood up and ordered me to go out. The one with the lantern went in front of me, leading the way. I followed him and we went into an underground room. We were later joined by two others. In the room I noticed two poles and a horizontal pole. This did not immediately mean anything to me. I was ordered to undress myself. At first I refused and demanded an explanation. They went and collected some sticks, and they started beating me while I was undressing myself. They took a rope and tied my hands to the horizontal pole. My legs were tied together and they then tied them to the other pole, which caused a lot of pain in my back, and they beat me with the sticks until I fell unconscious.

They then took me to the room and this was repeated throughout two months. Then I was transferred to another place, where I was again confronted with these questions: 'Where, when and by whom were you recruited to be a South African spy, and what did they promise you?' I told them that I was never recruited. This was the first time that anybody had even intimated why I was being treated like a criminal. I told them that I joined SWAPO to fight for the freedom of our country, and that I never had any connection with the South African regime.

I told them that I was very well known, especially in the place where I came from, Luderitz, and at our school in Omaruru. I was sure they could get a lot of information about my political activities from those places. But they had written off our high school as a training ground for South African spies! Therefore they didn't trust any student coming from that school.

They took out their ropes and a black cloth. They ordered me to undress, and the black cloth was tied round my eyes. This really scared me. I started shouting that they were going to kill an innocent person. They told me to go out, and because I was blindfolded somebody was holding me from behind. After walking for a distance I could feel that I was going in a type of underground, in a sort of hole. I was ordered to sit down flat on the ground and then I got a shower of sticks beating me. I didn't know where the next blow was coming from, and my hands were now tied as well. So they started beating while I was seated.

They ordered me to lie on one side and then after finishing they ordered me to lie on the other side and then again on my stomach and they kept on beating until they were tired. So I was in pain and they left me there and took off the blindfold. They left me in that hole and later every time I wanted to lift up my head I collapsed.

After I don't know how many hours I lifted up my head again and saw a girl sitting a distance from the hole. I asked her for water and she refused. It started raining and I was still in the hole. A male guard came and then he told me to go into a hut. By this time I could not walk because my whole body was swollen. So I had to crawl up to the hut. This interrogation continued like this, with beatings and solitary confinements, for eight months. After this eight months I could not bear the pain any more.

I really had confidence that justice would one day prevail and that the truth would come out. So I decided to make up a story. I knew that my story would be a lie. Maybe it would last for a month and then the truth would come out. Of course later I realised that that lie lasted for five full years, and maybe for the rest of my life because SWAPO has never shown any willingness to investigate the case. So I 'confessed' that I was a South African spy. I gave them impossible dates. I told them I was trained in Rehoboth, at the 'big building with writing on the front "South African Training Centre" — a place that does not even exist in Rehoboth. I gave them names of people who do not exist, but even then SWAPO did not investigate to find that this was a lie, leading me then to the conclusion that SWAPO was never interested in arresting enemy agents.

After I 'confessed' I was put together with other alleged enemy agents. We were sleeping in a dug-out. Then there were about 30 of us. This number grew to over 100. The dug-out is a hole dug in the ground with a layer of three bricks round the edge. Usually it was so overcrowded that we had to arrange ourselves in lines facing different ways to find the space to sleep. During the day, when we were not forced to do hard labour outside we had just enough space to sit down on the ground. The roof was made of corrugated iron. It

HOW SWAPO TORTURED ITS OWN FIGHTERS

was very hot. There were small holes which served as windows with iron bars. In that dug-out everything was done. Once the door was closed it was the toilet and the eating room. It was also the hospital at the same time. Small tins were used for the toilet.

There were diseases like asthma and bronchitis, beri-beri, skin diseases and some peculiar stress illnesses. There were many people who suffered mental illness. One woman gave birth in the hole, without water, without scissors, without so much as a clean cloth to lay the baby on. The baby died, the mother was taken away — and was put back in the hole after a couple of days.

I remained in this place until May 1989 (that was almost five years from the time I was first arrested in Cuba in November 1984). In all that time we had no chair, no bed. It was a privilege to get an empty rice sack to sleep on, or a milk drum to sit on outside the hole. We had nothing to read. We existed on talk about our childhood, and fantasies and dreams — to such an extent that we felt guilty if we did not dream because we would have nothing to tell the others.

Ndamona: I was ordered to go to one room where my hands and legs were tied and I was hung on a crossbar while they beat me severely with sticks and after a time I fell unconscious, but even when I recovered they started again, beating me.

They asked when, where and by whom was I recruited to work for the enemy? I gave a negative answer to all these questions, and my interrogators were not satisfied and they threatened to kill me. One of them took out his pistol and told me that this was the end of my life. But another — of course this is a strategy of theirs — came to my rescue and said: 'No! Give her more time to go and think. She will come to her senses.' Although I was severely beaten no medical treatment was granted to me. I was again taken out, and again they repeated the three questions, and I was beaten on the raw wounds and very special at this interrogation was the psychological torture they gave me.

They would come and wake me up in the middle of the night, tie my hands and tell me that this was the last day of my life. They asked me: 'Do you want to die, or do you want to tell us the truth?' I repeatedly said that I had no other truth to say. I would be sitting there waiting for any moment when I would be called out to be killed, and any footsteps in front of the door would mean to me that the time of my death had arrived.

I went through this treatment for three months. Then I was transferred to another jail called Etale. Here I was beaten severely and other types of torturing methods were also used on me. For example, they had two thick sticks and they would put the ends together and tie them and then they would insert my head (around the temple area) between these two sticks and then they would tie the other end of the sticks so that they were clamped tightly around my head. While I was in this position they would be beating me.

Or they take a bow string and tie it around one of my fingers and pull it so tight that it would bite into the flesh of my finger. After that I would lose the feeling in my finger for a couple of months — it just went dead. I stayed in this camp for eight months and because I didn't confess to being an enemy agent I was transferred to another jail called Hainyeko. There I underwent torture and interrogation and after three months I just decided that I had to give them what they want, hoping that the truth would come out one day. The camp guards could beat us at any time. For example on 11 November 1986 they cooked up a story against me that I planned to run away from prison and I was beaten up severely, and again no medical treatment was given to me.

Our main cry to the SWAPO leadership is to release those who are still languishing in their dungeons in Angola and elsewhere. The SWAPO leaders have said they are not holding prisoners any more, but we are aware that some of those people with whom we were in prison are not in the country to participate in the so called 'free and fair' election. The SWAPO leadership must give an account of the whereabouts of these innocent Namibians.

'A PLACE WHERE YOU ARE GOING TO SLEEP...'
A NAMIBIAN STORY

After being imprisoned and tortured by the South African state for his trade union and SWAPO activities, Henry Boonside was one of hundreds of Namibian fighters to experience the shock of unexpected detention, torture and interrogation by his own party. In this interview, he explains what happened to him and his comrades, and discusses the corruption of the SWAPO leadership and the treacherous role of the Soviet Union.

Henry Boonside was a SWAPO trade unionist who organised the first Mineworkers' Union at Rossing. In 1977 and 1978 he was detained by the South African security police for short periods for his union activities. Towards the end of 1978 Henry organised a strike at Rossing, where the miners had been cheated of a promised pay rise. 'All the workers were involved', said Henry. 'The plant was virtually at a standstill. They had to employ the whites at double the salaries for the period the strike lasted.'

During the strike a bakery was blown up. The bombers were not identified, but Henry and another comrade, Pickering, were arrested and tortured for three weeks by the South African police. Aged 26, Henry spent a year in prison. On his release in October 1979 he worked for SWAPO as the full-time organiser of the National Union of Namibian Workers.

'So many organisations throughout the world had been supporting this non-existent trade union organisation in Namibia. There were no workers; it was not functioning at all. There was no office to talk about. There was not even a constitution. There was only me and Pickering who started to organise the workers.'

They organised the first mineworkers' union in Namibia, then the Transport and Allied Workers' Union and the Engineering Workers' Union.

Henry was invited by SWAPO leader John Ya Otto to visit Botswana and then to accompany him to Zambia to attend the first graduation ceremony of Namibian students studying at the United Nations Institute. Upon his return to Namibia he was stopped by the South African police and charged with possession of banned publications (about 57 Marxist books).

'That very same afternoon I was taken back to court. The case against me was withdrawn and I was re-arrested under Article 6 of the Terrorism Act and transferred to Pretoria, where I went through a lot of torture. I was questioned — where the SWAPO bases are, what SWAPO bases I visited during my stay in Zambia. Well, I didn't visit any bases in Zambia. I was tortured, kicked, beaten in the stomach, and I went through electric shocks.'

Henry went on hunger strike to demand his release and was eventually found guilty of being in possession of banned publications. Fearing a long prison sentence, as he already had a suspended sentence, Henry decided to flee the country. With the approval of his trade union and SWAPO comrades, he took his wife and children to join SWAPO leader Sam Nujoma in exile on 1 May 1980.

Nujoma welcomed him: 'I am very happy that you have decided to join us abroad. We are aware of your hard work in Namibia and we hope that you are going to work harder . . . If only more people of your calibre could come to join us here . . . If more educated people like you' — Henry studied law but never practised — 'could join us we would be very happy . . . You have to go for military training prior to you being assigned to any department. Your military training will only take three months because officials only do three months' military training.' Henry told him he was prepared to do any kind of work, 'so long as I know that I can contribute to the struggle of the Namibian people to free my country'.

He worked for six weeks for John Ya Otto, SWAPO secretary for Labour, drafting a constitution for the National Union of Namibian Workers. Things changed soon after Henry set off for basic military training. 'I was welcomed to Lubango by the ex-SWAPO Secretary of Defence Peter Nanyemba. His last words were: "I am not going to send you back because my department also needs educated people like you."

'I was taken to a camp — Ongulunmbashia, not far from the military training centre. I was given a bed, whereupon I told the driver I never brought any blankets. He said he would go and collect blankets for me. Upon his return he said: "The guy from the storeroom is not there so I cannot give you blankets, but I will take you to a place where you are going to sleep for the night."

'The place I was taken on the night of 21 June 1980 (I never forget the date) was a prison.'

He had expected to join others waiting for training. When he went in, the others asked: 'Are you Namibian?' and 'What did you do?' This was the first indication he had that he was in a prison. 'I did not have blankets, and they were sleeping under sacks. Others had torn blankets. The people were all there because they had committed a crime — drinking, stealing, fighting, raping (rape was quite common). That Sunday morning we were taken out for training, and I refused to go out.

'At lunch-time food was brought, just this yellow hard porridge and beans. There were some maggots floating on top of the sauce. Being just from home, I thought if this is the struggle I will just have to get used to it, but I cannot now, it will take some time. I just could not take it, and I was also very much demoralised.'

Henry tried to escape, but was caught. 'I was tied by my hands and feet to a tree. They started stripping me. I had marks on my body, wounds from previous torture. They asked me: "Where is the communication the South African government sent you with?"

'I told them: "I am not hiding anything." It pained me very much inside that they were asking me this. I said: "No, it is better for you to bring another ten ropes and tie me to this tree, because I am not going into that prison. I might as well die here." '

Eddy Nekongo from Brazzaville, from SWAPO headquarters, told Henry that he might die of cold, and SWAPO would get the blame. So out of loyalty he agreed to go into the prison.

He described the dungeon, a hole about three metres deep in the ground, with a roof supported by pillars. 'There were two guards standing next to the centre pole and there was a chain as big as could pull a truck. One end of that chain was tied around the centre pole with a padlock. They grabbed me from behind, these two guards, and the other guys grabbed my feet. The other end of that chain was tied around my right leg with a padlock.

'That is where I remained for four months, like a dog. I was forced later even to tear my underpants from my body because they were so full of lice. For that four months I had about a metre and a half radius to move. And I was made to eat there, sleep there, to help myself to do whatever a human being must do just there. Well, I could at least wipe my body with a little water I was given — a tin of about two and a half litres — but take off the trousers I could not. I was made to stay in those trousers for four months.'

From June to November, Henry was not told why he was in prison. Then they took him out and said: 'Today you are going to write your life story from the day you were born up to the day you came to this place.' Henry remembers: 'I wrote that 50 times during my stay there, and every time they were saying: "No, this is not right. You know what we want to know." '

He was taken to another prison, stripped, tied and beaten savagely with a bundle of sticks for two hours. 'Today', they told him, 'you are going to tell us who recruited you, when you were recruited, what type of training you had, who sent you here to come spying on SWAPO, how long was your mission, and what type of mission you came for.'

'It went on like that for about six weeks,' said Henry. 'One day they would beat you, the next day they would not. Just like that. Torturing you mentally as well as physically. I was even once put in

'A PLACE WHERE YOU ARE GOING TO SLEEP...' 43

a dug-out in a small hole about a metre square and then a corrugated sheet was put on top and they made fire on the top.'

After this treatment, Henry concluded his life was in danger and decided to make up a story. 'So I said: "OK, I was sent by the South Africans on a diplomatic mission to come and gather information as to what SWAPO is planning in the diplomatic sphere. It was possible that SWAPO might send me as a diplomatic representative to western Europe, and then I would be in a position to pass this information on to the South African embassy or, if not, to an American embassy." I was made to confess on a tape, on paper.'

They came back and demanded names of his supposed contacts in SWAPO. Henry was beaten for a week, but refused to implicate John Ya Otto as they seemed to want. Henry and about 60 others remained in the prisons they were forced to build. He described one prison called Etale where there is a deep water-hole.

'Those dungeons are unbelievable. There are no vents at all. Sealed off completely. There is only an oblong left about the size of a door where the ladder is, used in the morning and at lunch-time to give us food and in the evenings again for us to relieve ourselves. They are opening at about six in the morning and closing that hole about three in the afternoon. From three you stay there in the darkness. The little air that comes in comes from the oblong, and this is covered with a corrugated sheet. The little holes left there are where air comes through for more than 50 people. The space you have at your disposal there is about two by five (ten square feet). It's so overcrowded and so hot that whether it's winter or summer you can never sleep with a blanket.'

Henry spent about four years there, from 1981 to 1985. He saw about seven of his comrades die. Prisoners were constantly moved from one prison to another. Some were transferred to unknown places. Henry and his comrades campaign now to demand to know from SWAPO what became of them.

Towards the end of 1986 Henry was moved to a prison where there were about eight very big holes taking anything from 36 to 96 people. Leaders were kept separately in small holes. One of the

SWAPO leaders imprisoned there, Henry said, was Victor Nkandi. He was sentenced to death by South Africa, but freed on appeal. He went into exile, only to be named as a spy and to die in prison there.

In April 1986 140 people were transferred from prison to an unknown destination just a week before Sam Nujoma visited the prisons. Henry reported Nujoma's message to the prisoners:'I greet you in the name of our great forefathers' — he mentioned all those great leaders who shed their lives for freedom. 'I don't know why you love money, why you love nice things. You are prepared to betray the Namibian revolution for nice cars, for money, for farms, for white women, etc.

'Your mothers gave birth to spies, betrayers of the Namibian revolution. You are kept here in the dungeons until after independence. Whereupon you will be paraded in front of the Namibian nation and your heads will be chopped off by the Namibians for your deeds.'

On 10 January 1989 the SWAPO administrative secretary, Moses Garoeb, told the prisoners they were to be released and reintegrated into the Namibian community in Angola.

On 19 April 1989 the SWAPO chief of security, Solomon Auala, ('Jesus'), announced they would be moved. Henry calls him the most corrupt and the most feared man in SWAPO. 'This man has been responsible for the deaths of many, many people. He started by killing Namibians way back with the Shipanga rebellion. He was the one who was ordered by Moses Garoeb to shoot, then to come and report whoever was shot by him. That man was one of the key men in the SWAPO spy drama, and is feared even by Nujoma. People like Nujoma, Moses Garoeb, and others, they are involved in a lot of killings and a lot of corruption, and the one is aware of what the other did, so that the one cannot expose the other. If one exposed the other then he would be exposed and so the chain would go on.'

Henry pointed out that many of the leaders of SWAPO are from the Kwanyamas, the strongest clan of the Ovambo people. They emerged as the most powerful group in the SWAPO leadership after the death of Nanyemba.

'On 18 May 1989 we were visited by Herman Toivo ja Toivo, the

SWAPO secretary general. He informed us of the central committee's decision to release us. We were also given two options: to be reintegrated into SWAPO; or to be handed over (as it was put by him) to the South African racist regime — our masters by whom we were sent to come and destroy SWAPO!

'They said in the days when they arrested me I was "never a SWAPO member". So now how can I be reintegrated into SWAPO after not ever being a member of SWAPO? How can a spy be reintegrated into SWAPO? But the second option was completely unacceptable because we are not spies of South Africa. How can I agree to be handed over to South Africa when I know I am not a spy?'

Henry described what 'reintegration' meant.

'We couldn't communicate with other people in other bases, but at least we were given beds, blankets, decent clothes, cups and knives and forks. It comes as a very big surprise to go from one extreme to the other. We had been walking barefoot; we only had a vest with short sleeves throughout the year; the food was horrible. Now, all of a sudden, we were put in a palace. We had everything at our disposal. We could eat three times a day. We could change clothes when we wished. We had a nice roof over our heads.'

A senior army commander of the UN Technical Advisory Group (UNTAG) forces came to interview the detainees, but he never relayed their messages to the Angolan authorities.

The next day's visit by a group of so-called international journalists was no better at getting the truth to the world. 'Most of them were in fact pro-SWAPO journalists. There was a TV crew from France, a TV crew from west Germany, a journalist from Cuba, a journalist from the Soviet Union, a crew from Angola, and two journalists from Namibia — of course from the pro-SWAPO press of Namibia. What we did was show them the scars on our bodies. We did that as individuals although we had agreed as a group not to speak to them as individuals. We stripped ourselves and we showed them how we were tortured.

'That very same afternoon 'Jesus' came with a truck full of soldiers. They jumped off the truck as if they were coming to rearrest us. I can tell you that day I must have run the world record for the fastest 1,000 metres! I ran about 25 kilometres. We all ran away because we thought they were going to rearrest us.'

Everything was taken from them, and they fled to the bush, from where they were able to send four volunteers to contact the UN and the Angolans.

But the Angolan authorities didn't want them to go back to Namibia. One social welfare worker made this explicit. 'She one day said to us that if we allow you people to return to Namibia you are going to take away, each one of you, your immediate families, your relatives. You, each one of you, will take away 2,000 supporters from SWAPO with what you are going to tell them.'

Instead they were offered scholarships and work to stay in Angola. The detainees went to the UN and the International Red Cross, demanding action. It was only after threats of sit-ins and hunger strikes that they were allowed back to Namibia on 4 July. Henry is convinced he owes his life to the pressure of the Parents' Committee.

He explained his views on the future of Namibia.

'SWAPO can never bring true freedom to this country. In 1981 there was hunger in the SWAPO settlements in Angola. Many people died in the SWAPO settlements. But at the SWAPO headquarters in Luanda there were very big storerooms, there was a lot of food being wasted, while people were dying in the settlements. Even just to bring a few bags of meal was a problem. They cannot even organise that. There are still people who think that they can rule this country while they cannot even see to the well-being of a handful of Namibians outside the country. The same leaders who claim to be revolutionaries are the ones sleeping with children aged 14, and they are the very ones who are sending married men away from their wives so that they themselves can sleep with the wives.'

He told us about some of the many crises in SWAPO, starting with the rebellion of soldiers in Tanzania in the 1960s against mismanagement that meant people had nothing to eat and didn't have uniforms. 'They called in the Tanzanian army to crush that rebellion.'

He spoke then of Shipanga. 'You know what the SWAPO leadership did? They feared that so many people were getting educated and coming home this would pose a very big threat to the SWAPO leadership because they themselves were uneducated. Even a person like Nujoma in the past used to fight with a carbine, but he doesn't know that we are now fighting with automatic weapons. He did not keep pace with developments. They regarded these fellows as a very big threat to their position as leaders of SWAPO.

'There were also some other grievances: SWAPO never had a constitution; and they said Nujoma was never elected in a congress, and how come Nujoma is the leader of SWAPO? They were demanding an immediate congress and that a constitution be drafted. Instead, a commission was set up. Andreas Shipanga was labelled as the chief instigator. He was imprisoned. Thousands of innocent Namibian children were killed by Jesus Auala. Thousands of people were killed by people like this Moses Garoeb. They were the ones.

'In the past if you were labelled as a spy you would just be shot — you were killed. We were lucky: we were detained, although many of our fellow inmates must have been killed. They are missing to this day. A commission of inquiry was set up. But Nujoma is busy reorganising his party. Nujoma is a tribalist. He is not bothered about Namibia as a whole.

'In order for the SWAPO leadership to keep people's minds from the inner problems of SWAPO it was necessary for them to create something to keep people in suspense. That is what they did by saying: do not trust your brother, even the person standing next to you. Even your shadow might be a spy, so be careful. That mistrust was deliberately created you see.'

Henry emphasised the role of Stalinism in the corruption of the SWAPO leadership.

'The Soviet Union had experts in all the SWAPO departments in Angola. They cannot say that they were not aware of what was going on. Some of them even remarked to people who were later apprehended, that you Africans have no brains. You are now busy destroying yourselves. People are just disappearing from the camps.'

Henry cites the visit of one Soviet prosecutor in 1983. Prisoners told him they were innocent and were beaten savagely. 'I am sure that those under technical cover from the Soviet Union in those departments of SWAPO are responsible. They are supposed to write reports to their immediate superiors in the Soviet Union every month. Do you mean to tell me they never wrote reports to their leaders? It is impossible. The Soviet Union granted SWAPO some semi-diplomatic status in 1988 while there was a cry going on for our release.'

Both Cuba and Bulgaria imprisoned Namibian comrades and sent them back under military escort.

'One guy had to defend his master's thesis in Bulgaria just the day before his apprehension. That guy was just taken and put into prison for a few days and then flown to Angola under Bulgarian intelligence custody. It is well known that the Soviet Union supplies arms to the governments to use against the people. The Soviet Union gave arms to Idi Amin to kill his own people. They never said anything against Amin. Only when he was crushed finally did they turn against Amin. The same with SWAPO. I would not be surprised if the whole method of interrogation and torture was devised in the Soviet Union.'

MEETING SURVIVORS

After the Budapest conference in 1990 I returned to Britain along with the comrades from South Africa and Namibia who had gone to the conference. Looking through the newspapers one morning, we read an article about a group of South Africans in Kenya who claimed they were the survivors of a mutiny in MK (Umkhonto we Sizwe, the ANC armed wing) based in Angola in 1984. The article said that the mutiny had been in protest at the lack of democracy inside the liberation army and that the ANC's 'security forces' had crushed it with great brutality. The Namibians immediately set about making contact with the people in Kenya.

In July 1990 I travelled to South Africa and spent time with Bongani in Durban. By this time he had the telephone number of a refugee hostel in Nairobi where the South African 'mutineers' were living. He contacted them and made arrangements for me to fly up and see them.

I was met by five men who took me back to their hostel. They had only recently got accommodation there after managing to collar a visiting South African church leader and ANC member and persuading him to arrange for them to be given somewhere to stay. For months they had been living rough in Nairobi's central park, begging for money to stay alive. Before that, following their resignation and flight from an ANC camp in Tanzania, they had wandered from place to place without money or identity papers, ending up in prison in several different countries. Now they had food and a bed, and they set about writing down an account of the mutiny. In the hostel they also had the chance to talk to several students who had recently returned from Russia and were able to report on all the events of perestroika and the transformation of most of the leading members of the Soviet Communist Party into advocates of capitalism. This helped the ANC soldiers, who had all done military training in eastern Europe, to make more sense of the terrible events they had lived through.

What follows are some short interviews I did with some of the ANC soldiers and then their own account of their fight for the armed wing to take up an effective fight against apartheid.

Bob Myers
June 1997

'TORTURE BECAME A SYSTEM'
INTERVIEWS WITH ANC FIGHTERS
(1990)

Former soldiers of the African National Congress campaign against the organisation's leadership, who used torture and killings to silence internal dissent. ANC leader Nelson Mandela promised action on the former ANC fighters' demand that leaders who used repressive methods be brought to justice — but nothing has been done. Here two of the ANC ex-detainees talk about how they first joined the ANC and what they think of it now.

Luvo Mbengo: We saw what the ANC was really like

I am from Port Elizabeth. In 1978, after the events of the 16 June uprising, I was shot by the police in St. George's Square. I was at secondary school. The same year I was arrested and charged. I got six lashes. In 1979 I joined the Congress of South African Students and the black consciousness movement in Port Elizabeth. In 1980 we organised a school boycott and I was arrested for attending an illegal gathering.

In the same year I left with friends to join the ANC in Lesotho, in order to defend ourselves against the regime. In 1981 I was in ANC camps in Angola. In 1982 I was sent to the Soviet Union for special military training and security service training. I spent a year in the Soviet Union, then returned to Angola.

During this period there were complaints about the ANC security service: beatings, torture, arrests of those who wanted to go home to fight, and secret killings of members. I joined in these protests. I wanted to go home and fight. And I wanted a conference of the ANC to solve these problems.

Luvo then tells the story of the uprisings in the camps and his imprisonment in the notorious Quatro prison, the ANC concentration camp.

On release from prison in Tanzania, after we went on hunger strike, we sneaked over the border to Kenya. Now we realised that this brutality in the ANC was the nature of the organisation. We wanted democracy. They could kill all of us, but we were sure history would prove us right. After the changes in eastern Europe we had still more confidence that we were right. We realised that in the ANC the method of killing people and other things were connected with politics in eastern Europe.

Now we were prepared to die for the struggle. Mandela says that his life has been dedicated to a struggle to fight white domination and I too am prepared to die for it. The ANC regarded us as just followers, not members. We are not following the leadership. We are following the policies of fighting apartheid.

Bandile Ketelo: The ANC torturers are still there

I was born in 1957 in the eastern Cape. I started to be active in politics in Hilltown high school. Hilltown was run by whites, and there one came into direct contact with the apartheid system at school. Before that I had little idea of apartheid practices. I participated in black consciousness activities and helped set up the South African students' movement. I was an executive committee member.

Clashes between Hilltown students and the authorities led to a strike in October 1975. As a result of that strike I was expelled. In February 1976 I was arrested by the South African security branch. Most of my colleagues had been arrested during the holidays. I was detained at Fort Glamorgan in East London and released after two weeks' interrogation.

TORTURE BECAME A SYSTEM

I now continued my studies by post, but as I knew the racist police would come for me again I decided to escape from South Africa. My first escape was on my own initiative. At that time there were no structures of the ANC in South Africa. I left with a friend who had relatives in Namibia. We went there to make contact with South West Africa People's Organisation to help me cross to the liberation movement. But the family in Namibia were not happy to have me. They were afraid. So I left before I could make contact with anyone. I met so many problems I had to go back to South Africa by hiking on my own. I remained underground until the following year. I knew it would not last long. The police would track me down.

In July 1977 I had problems with the South African security forces again, so I decided to leave the country again. Now I had made contact with a former prisoner on Robben Island. But he did not know any way out of the country. This time I left with two friends. I have heard that both of them are dead: one died in combat and one of sickness.

We had contacts in Namibia who could put us in touch with SWAPO. The SWAPO office did not want to help us slip out of the country. They handed us over to a priest, a SWAPO sympathiser. He hid us in a church until contacts were made with people who took us to Botswana. We handed ourselves over to the police and were in prison until we were taken to Francistown. We joined the ANC and went to the camps in Angola. I trained in guerrilla warfare and had some introduction to the politics of the ANC and to Marxism.

In 1979 some problems developed in the camps. Most of the cadres wanted to go home. We were engaged in training for war and felt we were ready to face the conditions back in South Africa. But we found we were being given more and more training that was endless. We decided no, man, this was too much. We wanted to go back and fight. This led to the uprising in the camps. The ANC crushed the uprising. It was during this time that Quatro was built.

Bandile reported years of beatings and torture at the hands of the ANC.

Finally these matters reached the people of South Africa. We all know what Comrade Mandela's response was. He admitted that these things happened. Now I feel that this is not the proper way of tackling the situation. Comrade Mandela is missing the point in some way. The tortures did not start in response to our mutiny.

We are dealing with a situation where torture had become a system of operation of the ANC security. There had been many instances where comrades died. There were people who were tortured back in 1981. The mutiny was in 1984. Two comrades were beaten to death by security in 1978. A comrade was arrested in 1979 and to this day we do not know where he is. It is my sincere belief that this comrade died. So the tortures were not confined to one episode. Comrade Mandela is wrong. Again, he comes up with the idea that these issues were dealt with immediately. This is a distortion, whether deliberate or not. The people who were involved in these things are still in ANC security at the ANC headquarters in South Africa. So what does he mean they were dealt with?

In December 1989 two comrades escaped from the ANC in Tanzania and reported to the Tanzanian police the forms of torture used against them: tying string around their testicles and other brutal ways of inflicting pain. So when Mandela says they dealt with this in 1984 he is wrong. And when some of our comrades returned to South Africa, Sisulu issued a statement saying these six comrades had come back to report to their masters, insinuating that our comrades were enemy agents.

But in 1989 in Tanzania we presented Sisulu with a document detailing everything that had gone on in the ANC since the Soweto uprisings. So he knew everything. In spite of that he decided to call our comrades enemy agents.

Shortly after Sisulu's statement one of the returning exiles was murdered after leaving an ANC office.

A MISCARRIAGE OF DEMOCRACY
THE ANC SECURITY DEPARTMENT IN THE 1984 MUTINY IN UMKHONTO WE SIZWE

Five former fighters in Umkhonto we Sizwe, the ANC's military wing, Bandile Ketelo, Amos Maxongo, Zamxolo Tshona, Ronnie Massango and Luvo Mbengo, wrote this account of the 1984 mutiny.

Prelude to mutiny

On 12 January 1984, a strong delegation of ANC National Executive Committee members arrived at Caculama, the main training centre of Umkhonto we Sizwe (MK) in the town of Malanje, Angola. In the past, such a visit by the ANC leadership — including its top man, the organisation's president, Oliver Tambo — would have been prepared for several days, or even weeks, before their actual arrival. Not so this time. This one was both an emergency and a surprise visit.

It was not difficult to guess the reason. For several days, sounds of gunfire had been filling the air almost every hour of the day at Kangandala, near Malanje, and just about 80 kilometres from Caculama, where President Tambo and his entourage were staying. The combatants of MK had refused to go into counter-insurgency operations against the forces of the Union for Total Independence of Angola (UNITA) in the civil war in Angola and had defied the security personnel of the ANC. They had decided to make their voice of protest stronger by shooting randomly into the air. It was pointed out to all the commanding personnel in the area that the shooting was not meant to endanger anybody's life, but was just meant to be a louder call to the ANC leadership to address themselves afresh to the desperate problems facing our organisation.

Clearly put forward also was that only Tambo, the president of the ANC, Joe Slovo, the chief-of-staff of the army, and Chris Hani, then the army commissar, would be welcome to attend to these issues. An illusory idea still lingered in the minds of the MK combatants that most of the wrong things in our organisation happened without the knowledge of Tambo, and that given a clear picture of the situation, he would act to see to their solution.

Joe Slovo, now secretary of the South African Communist Party (SACP), had himself risen to prominence as a result of the daring combat operations which MK units had carried out against the racist regime. In 1983 the SACP quarterly, the *African Communist*, had carried an article by Slovo about J.B.Marks, another of the ANC/SACP leaders, who had died in Moscow in 1972. That article, emphasising democracy in the liberation struggle, was a fleeting glance into some of the rarely talked-of episodes in the proceedings of the Morogoro Consultative Conference of the ANC, held in Tanzania in 1969. It might have been written for a completely different purpose, but for the guerrillas of MK it was a call for active involvement in the solution of our problems.

Chris Hani was one of the veterans of the earliest guerrilla campaigns of the ANC in the Wankie area of Rhodesia, against the regime of Ian Smith, in 1967. He had had his name built by his 'heroic' exploits as he fictitiously escaped 'assassination attempts' against him carried out by the South African regime in Lesotho, where he had been head of the ANC mission. Despite these claims it is doubtful whether he could have survived over a decade in Lesotho (1972-82) if he had posed a threat as serious as those sometimes portrayed. Hani, it must be stressed, never carried out any major operations in South Africa, and there are no operations carried out in his name in the whole of MK combat history, unlike Joe Slovo, for instance.

A MISCARRIAGE OF DEMOCRACY 57

The guerrillas in Angola levelled their bitterest criticisms against three men in the NEC of the ANC, men who had had a much more direct involvement in the running of our army. The first was Joe Modise, army commander of the ANC since 1969. He was looked down upon by the majority of combatants as a man responsible for the failures of our army to put up a strong fight against the racist regime, a man who had stifled its growth and expansion. He was above all seen as someone who engaged himself in corrupt money-making ventures, abusing his position in the army.

The second was Mzwandile Piliso, the chief of security. He was then the most notorious, the most feared, soulless ideologue of the suppression of dissent and democracy in the ANC. The last one was Andrew Masondo, freed from Robben Island after 12 years of imprisonment, who had joined the ANC leadership in exile after the 1976 Soweto uprisings. In 1984 he was the national commissar of the ANC, and was therefore responsible for supervision of the implementation of NEC decisions and political guidance of the ANC personnel. Masondo was to use this responsibility to defend corruption, and was himself involved in abuse of his position to exploit young and ignorant women and girls. He was also a key figure in the running of the notorious ANC prison camp known to the cadres as 'Quatro' ('Four' in Portuguese). It was nicknamed Quatro after the Fort, the rough and notorious prison for blacks in Johannesburg, known to everybody as 'No. 4'.

Such was the situation when Chris Hani, together with Joe Nhlanhla, then the administrative secretary of the NEC and now chief of security, and Lehlonono Moloi, now chief of operations, arrived in Kangandala under instructions from the NEC to silence the ever-sounding guns of the guerrillas. Chris Hani was suddenly thrown into confusion by the effusive behaviour of the combatants as they expressed their grievances, wielding AKs which they vowed never to surrender until their demands were met. What were these demands?

First, the soldiers demanded an immediate end to the war by the MK•forces against UNITA and the transfer of all the manpower used in that war to our main theatre of war in South Africa. Second, they demanded the immediate suspension of the ANC security apparatus, as well as an investigation of its activities and of the prison camp Quatro, then called 'Buchenwald' after one of the most notorious Nazi concentration camps. Last, they demanded that Tambo himself come and address the soldiers on the solution to these problems. All that Chris Hani could do in this situation was to appeal for an end to random shootings in the air, and to appeal to the soldiers to await the decision of the NEC after he had sent it the feedback about his mission.

The beginnings of Quatro

The demands mentioned above had far-reaching political implications for the ANC, which had managed to win high political prestige as the future government of South Africa. But for anyone to appreciate their seriousness, one must go back to the history of the ANC following the arrival of the youth of the Soweto uprisings to join the ANC. This historical approach to the mutiny of 1984 is more often than not deliberately neglected by the ANC leadership whenever they find themselves having to talk about this event. More than anything else, they fear the historical realities which justify this mutiny and show it to have been inevitable, given the genuine causes behind it.

The mainspring of the 1984 mutiny, known within the ANC as Mkatashingo, was the suppression of democracy by the ANC leadership. This suppression of democracy had taken different forms at different times in the development of the ANC, and it had given birth to resistance from the ANC membership at different times, taking forms corresponding to the nature of the suppression mechanisms. We will confine ourselves to those periods that had become landmarks and turning points in this history.

The first such remarkable events of resistance to the machinations of the ANC leadership were in 1979 at a camp known among South Africans as Fazenda, but whose actual name was Villa Rosa, to the north of Quibaxe, in northern Angola. The majority of the trained personnel of MK had been shifted from Quibaxe in November 1978 to occupy this camp, where they were expected to undergo a survival course to prepare for harsh conditions of rural guerrilla warfare. With the promise that the course would take three months, after which the combatants would be infiltrated back into South Africa to carry out combat missions, everybody took the course in their stride and with high morale.

After the first three months and the introduction of a second course, it became crystal clear that we were being fooled, to keep us busy. Voices of discontent began to surface in certain circles of the armed forces. The main cause of discontent was the suppression of our uncontrollable desire to leave Angola and enter South Africa to supplement the mass political upsurges of the people. Alongside this were also complaints about inefficiency of the front commanders and suspicions that they were treacherously involved in the failure of many missions, leading to the mysterious death of our combatants in South Africa.

Mzwandile Piliso was accused of over-emphasising the security of our movement against the internal enemy, at the expense of promoting comradely relations among the armed forces. He was promoting unpopular lackeys within the army while suppressing those who fell to his disfavour, branding them as enemy agents who would 'rot in the camps of Angola'.

The late Joe Gqabi [assassinated in Harare in 1981, while ANC representative in Zimbabwe] attended one such explosive meeting and commended the soldiers for their spirit of openness and criticism. Fazenda was getting out of hand, and the feeling of discontent began to spill into certain nearby ANC bases. Something had to be done to stamp down this resistance. The security organ of the ANC, which till then had just been composed of a few old cadres of the 1960s, began to be reorganised in all the camps. Young men from our own generation who had recently undergone courses in the Soviet Union and east Germany were spread into all the camps. It was during this time that construction of a prison camp near Quibaxe was speeded up, which later took the form of the dreaded Quatro. ANC general meetings, which were held weekly, and had been platforms for criticism and self-criticism, were now terminated.

The very first occupants of Quatro prison were three men from Fazenda: Ernest Khumalo, Solly Ngungunyana and Drake, who had defiantly left Fazenda to go to Luanda, where they hoped to meet the ANC chief representative, Max Moabi, to demand their own resignation from the ANC. The ANC did not accept resignation of its membership. Worse still, this was in Angola, a country where lawlessness reigned. After being beaten in a street in Luanda by ANC and Angolan security, they were bundled into a truck and taken straight to Quatro. Solly was released after two years, Ernest in 1984; Drake's end is still unknown. The camp remained highly secret within the ANC. Everyone sent to work there as a security guard undoubtedly had to have proved his loyalty to Mzwandile Piliso, and was expected not to disclose anything to anybody. Even among the NEC, the only ones who had access to Quatro were Mzwandile Piliso, Joe Modise and Andrew Masondo.

An 'internal-enemy-danger' psychosis

To completely efface the spirit of resistance in Fazenda, the majority of the MK forces there were taken to Zimbabwe, where they fought alongside guerrillas of the Zimbabwe African People's Union (ZAPU) led by Joshua Nkomo, against the Smith forces as well as the guerrillas of the Zimbabwe African National Union (ZANU), led by Robert Mugabe. Many worthy fighters perished there. Fazenda camp was closed in 1980, and fighters there were distributed among the two main camps of the ANC, Pango and Quibaxe, both to the north of Luanda. The chapter on Fazenda was closed. But a burning urge to liberate South Africa, with the only language the Boers understood, the gun, could not be trampled on as contemptuously as that. Yet it had become very dangerous to raise even a voice against the leadership. The ANC had become divided into a force of the rank and file and that of the leadership clubbed together with the security apparatus, which had grown to such enormous levels that practically every administration of whatever ANC institution was run by the security personnel, and practically every problem was viewed as a security risk and an 'enemy machination'.

Electricity pylons carry power to factories and white areas. The only electric light in South Africa's townships come from the giant lamps casting light

Life for black workers in southern Africa has always been dominated by the hours spent each day travelling to work in the towns from the desolate townships which were always built miles away to keep the white areas white.

Living conditions range from shacks built of cardboard, packing cases or corrugated iron to better, more solid buildings — and even to Winnie Mandela's 'palace'.

Right: March in Windhoek campaigning for information about the fate of liberation fighters detained by SWAPO, during Namibia's 'independence' elections in 1989.

Below: 1989: a Workers Revolutionary Party of Namibia march against SWAPO's detentions

Left: Twins Ndamona and Panduleni Kali left their homes as teenage students to join SWAPO and fight for their country's liberation but were later arrested and imprisoned. They came to Britain to expose the crimes of SWAPO in a speaking tour. Their first meeting was at the House of Commons, London.

Below: The Kali twins at the home of Hewat Beukes, former member of the SWAPO Youth League and founder member of the Namibian Workers Revolutionary Party. The grills were placed over the window during the liberation struggle after a hand grenade was tossed into the house.

Above: Ex–ANC soldiers, who took part in the 1985 mutinies, at a hostel in Nairobi, Kenya, prior to their return to South Africa.

Above: Members of the Workers International stop for a break in a weekend 'stopover meeting'. This meeting, like all gatherings at the time, was illegal under the state of emergency laws in Natal.

Representatives from Namibia and South Africa at an International Trade Union Solidarity Campaign conference in London in 1992. Amos Moxongo, one of the authors of the pamphlet on the mutiny in the ANC is in the middle of the back row. Bongani Mkhungo is in the front, left.

In a bid to strengthen their repressive apparatus, Andrew Masondo created a security crack force in a camp known as Viana, near Luanda. This unit, known as ODP (People's Defence Organisation), was composed mainly of very young men or boys. Its tasks were to guard the ANC leadership when they paid visits to different camps, to enforce discipline and bash up any forms of dissent and 'disloyalty'. By this time, after the Fazenda events, the ANC leaders had begun to whip up an 'internal-enemy-danger psychosis,' and whenever they visited the camps they had to be heavily guarded. Worse still if it was Tambo who visited: the whole camp would be disarmed, and only the security personnel and those attached to it would be allowed to carry weapons.

The next hot spot for the ANC was in Zambia, where the headquarters of the ANC was based and where most of the leadership was living. This was in 1980. MK cadres, who had been drilled for months in 'communist ideology' of the Soviet-east European type to denounce all luxuries and accept the hazards of the struggle, here came into direct confrontation with the opposite way of life lived by the ANC leaders. It became clear that the financial support extended to the ANC was used to finance the lavish way of life of the ANC leadership. Corruption, involving rackets of car, diamond and drug smuggling, was on a high rise. The security department itself was rocked by internal dissent between those who supported a heavy-handed approach and the predominantly young cadres who opposed it.

There was also the burning problem of the insignificant progress made by our forces in South Africa, at a time when our people were alone locked into bitter mass struggles against the racists. This aspect was further complicated by the decision of the NEC to send back to Angola a batch of MK forces who had survived the war in Zimbabwe and were discovered by the provisional government authorities in the assembly points, disguised as ZAPU guerrillas. These guerrillas, still itching to go to South Africa and aware of the conditions in the camps in Angola, refused pointblank the instructions to return to Angola.

Faced with these and many other related problems, a meeting was arranged between the leadership and the representatives of the three detachments, the Luthuli, June 16 and Moncada detachments. Among their representatives, the June 16 Detachment was represented by Sidwell Moroka and Moncada by Timmy Zakhele, both of whom later ended up in Quatro. The June 16 Detachment advanced the proposal to hold a conference of the whole ANC membership where these issues could be settled democratically. This proposal, which had popular backing from the overwhelming majority of the young cadres, was rejected by the ANC leadership, which never accepts any idea that puts in question its competence and credibility to lead.

It was in the process of these discussions that a discovery of a spy network was disclosed and a clampdown on the 'ambitious young men who wanted to overthrow the leadership of Tambo' was put into operation. The ANC security went into full swing, detaining the so-called enemy spies and those who were proponents of the conference. It was said that this spy-ring was not only concentrated in Zambia, but was everywhere that the ANC had its personnel. Many of these young men — Pharoah, Vusi Mayekiso, Kenneth Mahamba, Oshkosh and others — were later known to have died under torture and beatings in Quatro prison camp. Others such as Godfrey Pulu, Sticks and Botiki were released years later, after torture and the failure of the security department to prove their treachery. Men who were bodyguards of President Tambo and were unwilling to continue serving in the notorious security organs were almost all sent to serve punishments in other camps in Angola. Sidwell Moroka, James Nkabinde (executed at Pango in 1984), David Ngwezana, Earl and others were among those men. The guerrillas from Zimbabwe who refused to return to Angola were flogged and beaten and were later smuggled into Angola.

After this clampdown, and with the majority of the membership panic-stricken, a strong entourage of ANC National Executive Committee members, including President Tambo, took the rounds in all ANC camps in Angola in February 1981. Appearing triumphant but with agonising apprehension, the ANC leadership addressed the cadres about a spy network that had besieged the

ANC, and emphasised the need for vigilance. Some awful threats were also thrown at 'enemy agents and provocateurs' by Piliso, who rudely declared in Xhosa '. . . I'll hang them by their testicles'.

Soon thereafter, a tape-recorded address by Moses Mabhida, the late general secretary of the SACP, was circulated, criticising dagga-smoking and illicit drinking in ANC camps, and calling for strong disciplinary measures to be taken against the culprits. Commissions to investigate these breaches of discipline were set up in April 1981 in every ANC establishment. They were supervised by camp commanders and security officers in all the camps, and all those implicated were detained, beaten and tortured to extract information.

The issue was treated as a security risk, an enemy manœuvre to corrupt the culprits' loyalty to the ANC leadership. Most of those arrested were known critics of the ANC leadership and were labelled as anti-authority. During the whole period of investigation they were tied to trees outside and slept there. In Camalundi camp in Malanje province, Oupa Moloi, who was head of the political department, lost his life during the first day of interrogation. Thami Zulu (the travelling name of Muzi Ngwenya), who was the camp commander, and who himself died in ANC security custody in 1989, addressed the camp detachments about the death of Oupa, threatening to kill even more of these culprits who, at that time, swollen and in excruciating pain, were lined up in front of the detachment. Zulu/Ngwenya died in the ANC security department's hands in 1989 for alleged poisoning.

In Quibaxe, Elik Parasi and Reggie were 'finished off' at the instruction of the camp commander, Livingstone Gaza, at a time when they were in severe pain with little hope of survival. Others like Mahlathini, one of the talented artists who was responsible for the composition of many of the first songs of the Amandla Cultural Ensemble, were taken from Pango to Quatro, where they met their death.

It is important to realise that most of these atrocities were carried out in the camps themselves, and not in the secrecy of Quatro, where only a few would know. The operation succeeded in its objectives. Fear was instilled and hatred for the ANC security crystallised. Every cadre of MK took full cover, and the security department was striding, threatening to pounce on any forms of dissent. Camps were literally run by the security personnel. Many underground interrogation houses were set up in all places where the ANC had its personnel, and underground prisons were established in the places known as 'R.C.' and Green House in Lusaka and at a place in Tanzania disguised as a farm near the Solomon Mahlango Freedom College (Somafco) at Mazimbu, the main educational centre of the ANC in exile. In Mozambique a detention camp was set up in Nampula where 'suspects' and those who pestered the leadership about armed struggle in South Africa were kept.

MK began to crack into two armies, the latent army of rebels which kept seething beneath the apparent calm and obedience, and the army of the leadership, their loyal forces. The former was struggling for its life, kicking into the future, but all its efforts were confined within the suffocating womb of the latter. Security personnel were first-class members of the ANC. They had the first preference in everything, ranging from military uniforms and boots right up to opportunities for receiving the best military, political and educational training in well-off institutions in Europe.

Face to face with this state of affairs, disappointment and disillusion set in and the cadres began to lose hope in the ANC leadership. The rate of desertion grew in 1982-83. There occurred more suicides and attempted suicides. The political commissars, whose task was to educate the armed forces about the ideological and moral aspects of our army, became despised as the protectors of corruption and autocracy. It became embarrassing to be in such structures. Cases of mental disturbance increased. This was mostly the case with the security guards of Quatro, rumoured by the cadres to be caused by the brutalities they unleashed against the prisoners. It was this worsening state of the cadres that made Tambo issue instructions in September 1982 to all the army units to discuss and bring forward proposals to the leadership about the problems in which the ANC was enmeshed.

A change of forms

Series of meetings followed and the MK cadres, thirsty to exploit this oasis of democracy which the ANC president had decided to have them taste, levelled bitter criticisms about the state of our organisation. Once again the issue of the need for a conference was put forward. Among the questions raised by the paper issued by Tambo was what our response would be if the South African military decided to attack Mozambique. Were we ready to lay down our lives for a common cause with the Mozambican people? This question was treated by the combatants in a simplistic way, for it bore no significance to the nature of the problems we were faced with in the ANC. But the answer to it was right, in that the cadres emphasised the importance of intensifying armed action in South Africa, rather than fighting in foreign territories.

The reasoning behind such an approach by the MK cadres stemmed from their realisation of the weakness of our army, both numerically and in relation to the quality of training. This was a time when the heroic Palestine Liberation Organisation guerrillas were locked into bloody battles against the invading Israeli army in Lebanon. One could not but call this to mind eight months later, when the overwhelming majority of our armed forces was mobilised for counter-insurgency operation against UNITA in the Malanje and Kwanza provinces. One could not but note the similarities when Tambo appealed to the MK forces to 'bleed a little in defence of the beleaguered Angolan people,' as he addressed the MK forces in preparation for launching a raid against the UNITA bases across the Kwanza River.

With the discussions over and papers from different camps submitted to the leadership, Masondo took rounds in all the camps expressing the disappointment of President Tambo about papers submitted from Pango camp and Viana. Claiming to be echoing the views of President Tambo, he said the papers were 'unreadable' and that Tambo had not expected that this opportunity would be used for launching attacks against the leadership and military authorities.

In April 1983, some structural changes were announced. The Revolutionary Council, adopted at the 1969 Morogoro Conference, was abolished by the NEC and a new body was set up, the Political Military Council (PMC). Announcements of personnel to staff the Political Council and the Military Council were also made. The mere mention that Joe Modise would remain the army commander demoralised many cadres, who had speculated that he would be sacked as commander after rumours that he had been arrested in Botswana for diamond dealing (some cadres were severely punished for circulating that account) and because of his dismal failure to lead our army into meaningful battles against the South African racist regime.

All the changes announced by the NEC became meaningless and a farce for the armed forces. Meaninglessness stemmed from the fact that the cadres had come to realise that the change of structures was not the main issue: the personnel that manned these positions had to be changed. Their farcical nature derived from realisation by the membership that these changes had been advanced to forestall any demands for a democratic conference where the NEC could be subjected to scrutiny. This contempt for the demands and ideas of the grassroots, at a time when the balance of forces was turning in disfavour of the leadership, could only have the result that the ANC would pay dearly for it. To understand this scornful behaviour, one needs to understand the deep-seated Stalinist ideological leanings of the ANC leadership. We will consider this later. For now, having briefly set out the general outline of the background to the 1984 mutiny, let us examine the course of events.

The mutiny at Viana

Having received a dressing down from the rebellious armed forces at Kangandala on 12 January 1984, and having been presented with a package of demands, Chris Hani sped back to Caculama where he delivered the news to Tambo and his NEC. During his address that afternoon in the camp at Caculama, which was composed overwhelmingly of new trainees, President Tambo felt the need to introduce his NEC to the recruits and to lay stress on certain political issues. Pointing at the NEC members on the rostrum, he said: 'This is the political leadership of the ANC . . . ', and suddenly

A MISCARRIAGE OF DEMOCRACY 67

turning his eyes to a man next to him, he declared: 'This man founded this army . . .', patting him on his shoulder. That man was Joe Modise, the man whom the armed forces, in their majority, were saying should be deposed.

Acclaimed as a man of wisdom, a man no one could match in the way he had led the ANC, President Tambo saw the need even at that hour to firmly entrench Joe Modise in the MK commanding position. Tambo did not see a need to respond to the calls of the cadres to come and address them, in spite of the fact that he was only an hour's drive away. But, perhaps, nobody knows about armed soldiers, and the life of the most important man must be secured. Tambo and his entourage left Caculama for Luanda that same evening, without having addressed even a message to the mutineers. No sooner had the NEC left for Luanda than mutiny began to grow to higher levels. The whole of the eastern front was engulfed in sounds of gunshots, and there were stronger demands for the closure of the front and the deviation of the whole manpower to a war against Pretoria. A few days later word came from the NEC that the front would be closed and that all the soldiers must prepare themselves to leave Malanje for Luanda, where they would meet with the ANC leadership. The first convoy of a truckload of guerrillas left, followed by a second the following day, all eager for the meeting which they expected to put the ANC on a new footing.

Located at the outskirts of the capital city, Luanda, the ANC transit camp of Viana had been evacuated of all personnel, who had been sent to an ANC area in Luanda to prevent contact with the mutineers. Strict orders were circulated by the ANC security personnel that nobody in the district of Luanda should visit Viana or have any form of contact with the mutineers. Guerrillas from the Malanje Front entered Viana in a gun salute, shooting in the air with all the weapons in hand. Later the security personnel in Viana, under the command of a man known as Pro — a former security guard at Quatro and then also a camp commander at Viana, also very notorious among the mutinying guerrillas — demanded that every soldier surrender his weapons, explaining the danger they posed to the capital. The demand was dismissed summarily with the reason that arms provided security for the mutineers against the reprisals the security department would launch, given that situation. Instead, all the security personnel within the premises of the camp were searched and disarmed, but never even once were they pointed at with weapons. The administration of the camp deserted to other ANC establishments in Luanda.

In one of the metal containers used for detention, a corpse was found with a bullet hole in the head. It was the body of Solly, one of the strong critics of the ANC military leadership. At some stage he had tasted the bitter treatment of the security department and had in the process got his mind slightly disturbed. At the news of the mutiny in Malanje he had become vociferous and fearless, and that was the mistake of a lifetime.

That same day, some crews of guerrillas volunteered to round up ANC establishments in Luanda to explain their cause and to understand the political positions of others. Even though this was a dangerous mission, given the mobility of the ANC security personnel in Luanda and the likely collaboration with them of FAPLA [armed forces of the Angolan state, controlled by the Popular Movement for the Liberation of Angola, MPLA], the task was fulfilled. That very same day again, people from all ANC establishments came streaming to Viana to join and support the mutineers. The efforts of the leadership to isolate the mutineers were shattered and they resorted to force by laying ambushes to attack those who were travelling to Viana with guns. In one such encounter, Chris Hani, with an AK submachine gun, made his appearance on the side of the loyalists by chasing and firing at those who wanted to join the mutineers. For the first time since the mutiny began, a series of mass meetings were held in an open ground in Viana. Everybody was allowed to attend, even members of the security department.

The demand for democracy

It was in these mass meetings that the political essence of this rebellion began to solidify. A committee was elected by the guerrillas themselves, to take control of the situation and serve as their

A MISCARRIAGE OF DEMOCRACY 69

representative in meetings with the leadership. This body, which became known as the Committee of Ten, was chaired by Zaba Maledza, the travelling name of Ephraim Nkondo, a former student at the University of the North at Turfloop. Zaba was a former black consciousness activist in the South African Students' Organisation (SASO) during the days of Steve Biko who had joined the ANC in exile during the early 1970s and served as one of the foremost propagandists in the ANC radio programmes alongside Duma Nokhwe. A brother to Curtis Nkondo, one of the leaders of the United Democratic Front (UDF) in South Africa, Zaba had landed in Quatro in 1980 after some disagreements with the ANC military leadership while working for the movement in Swaziland, and was released in 1982. He then rejoined the radio broadcasting staff of the ANC in Luanda, where his unwavering opposition to men like Piliso and Modise, and his clarity of mind, had earned him the respect of both friends and foes within the ANC, something which even the ANC security begrudgingly appreciated.

Other members of the Committee of Ten included: 1. Sidwell Moroka, also known as Mhlongo (Omry Makgoale), who was formerly Tambo's personal bodyguard and was one of the group of security personnel punished by being sent to Angola following a mop-up operation in Lusaka in 1981. At the outbreak of the mutiny he was the district chief of staff in Luanda; 2. Jabu Mofolo, who was at that time the political commissar of the Amandla Cultural Ensemble; 3. Bongani Matwa, formerly a camp commissar in Camalundi; 4. Kate Mhlongo, at that time part of the radio propaganda staff in Luanda; 5. Grace Mofokeng, also attached to the radio staff; 6. Moses Thema, a former student at the Moscow Party School and at that time serving as the head of the political department at Caxito camp; 7. Sipho Mathebula, formerly a battalion commander at the Eastern Front; 8. Khotso Morena (Mwezi Twala) and 9. Simon Botha.

Also adopted at those meetings was a set of demands addressed to the ANC National Executive Committee. They were:

1. immediate suspension of the Security Department and establishment of a commission to investigate its all-round activities.

Included here was also the investigation of one of the most feared secret camps of the ANC, Quatro;

2. a review of the cadre policy of the ANC to establish the missing links that were a cause for a stagnation that had caught up with our drive to expand the armed struggle;

3. to convene a fully representative democratic conference to review the development of the struggle, draw new strategies and have elections for a new NEC.

The demands were a backhand blow in the face of the ANC leadership. They threatened to explode the myth of a 'tried and tested' leadership. No wonder Chris Hani, in one of those tense and emotionally charged meetings, in bewilderment retorted: 'You are pushing us down the cliff! You are stabbing us at the back!' And like a cornered beast they used everything within their reach to destroy their opponents. Election of people to leadership positions was long preached and accepted as unworkable within the ANC. The last conference had been held in 1969 in Morogoro, and it had also come about as a result of a critical situation which threatened to break the ANC, and as a result of pressure from below. The very elevation of Oliver Tambo from the deputy presidency in 1977, something that never received support at Morogoro, was done behind the backs of the entire membership, without even prior discussion or announcement. Not that it did not have the support of the membership, but such decisions in a politically prestigious body such as the ANC needed at least a semblance of democracy, even if a sugar coating.

The demand for a conference had been diverted in 1981 through the discovery of a 'spy-ring', and all those who talked about it then feared even the word thereafter. When the same demand had been voiced out in 1982, the ANC leadership came out with its own fully worked-out changes and structures without the participation of the membership, even changing structures adopted at the past conference. And this time, as Joe Modise said later, a group of soldiers thought they could send the ANC leadership to a conference room 'at gunpoint'. Those demands were clearly unacceptable to the leadership.

Commission of Inquiry, and after

In anticipation of a heavy-handed reaction from the ANC leadership, the committee members felt it was necessary to secure protection by the people of South Africa and the world. Placards calling for a political solution and reading 'No to Bloodshed, We Need Only a Conference' were plastered on the walls of Viana camp. Journalists were called, but they were never given the slightest chance to get nearer the mutineers. Two men, Diliza Dumakude and Zanempi Sihlangu, both of them members of the radio propaganda staff, were intercepted by the security personnel and murdered while on their way to the studios of Radio Freedom.

While all this was happening, the presidential brigade of FAPLA (the Angolan army) was being mobilised and prepared to launch an armed raid on Viana. The decision was that the whole mutiny must be drowned in blood. The ANC could not be forced by soldiers to a conference hall 'at gunpoint'. Early the following day, the mutineers were woken by the noise of military trucks and armoured personnel carriers (APCs) as the forces of FAPLA encircled the camp. An exchange of fire ensued as the guerrillas retaliated to the attack with their arms. Shortly thereafter, shouts of 'Ceasefire' emerged from one of the firing positions and Callaghan Chama (Vusi Shange), one of the commanders of the guerrillas, rose out of a trench beseeching for peace. One MK combatant, Babsey Mlangeni (travelling name), and one FAPLA soldier were already dead and an Angolan APC was on the retreat engulfed in flame.

What followed were negotiations between the national chief of staff of FAPLA, Colonel Ndalo, and the Committee of Ten. An agreement was reached after lengthy discussions with the guerrillas, with the Angolans trying to convince them that there would be no victimisations. Weapons were surrendered to the FAPLA commanders and they promised to provide security for everybody who was in Viana, and that even the ANC security would be disarmed. Two member of the OAU Liberation Committee arrived together with Chris Hani, who delivered a boastful address denouncing the whole mutiny and its demands as an adventure instigated by disgruntled elements. Then the usual political rhetoric followed, that the ANC was an organisation of the people of South Africa, and that those mutineers were not even a drop in an ocean and that the ANC could do without them. To demonstrate this, Hani called on all those who were still committed to serve as ANC members to move out of the hall. The hall was left empty. All the mutineers were still committed to the ideals of the ANC, they were committed to ANC policies. Nevertheless, they could discern deviations from the democratic norms proclaimed in those policy documents and declared on public platforms. It was a concern for this that had forced them to use arms in conditions where criticism of the leadership and democratic election of NEC members by the rank and file were branded as counter-revolutionary.

During the period of these events, another rebellion was breaking out in Caculama, the very camp in which President Tambo had delivered his address about the illegitimacy of the mutiny which had then been in progress in Kangandala. Some groups of trained guerrillas and officers, including the staff unit commissar, Jacky Molefe (the travelling name of Bandile Ketelo), moved out of the camp, boarding trucks and trains to join and support the mutineers at Viana. The training programme for the new recruits came to an abrupt stop, and this was another slap in the face of the ANC leadership because Caculama camp was their last hope to counterbalance the popularity of the mutiny. With the support from Caculama, the mutiny acquired a 90 per cent majority among the whole trained forces of MK in Angola, which was then the only country where the ANC had guerrilla camps.

The Angolan government authorities played a very dishonest role thereafter. They began to throttle this popular unrest in collaboration with the ANC security, dishonouring all the agreements they had made with the guerrillas. The security personnel of the ANC were allowed to enter the camp armed, which was defended by the Angolan armed forces with their weapons. Later Joe Modise and Andrew Masondo arrived, together with five men from headquarters in Lusaka. The five men, James Stuart, Sizakhele Sigxashe, Tony Mongalo, Aziz Pahad and Mbuyiselo Dywili, were introduced as a Commission of Inquiry set up on the

A MISCARRIAGE OF DEMOCRACY 73

instructions of Oliver Tambo to examine the whole episode. The following day, 16 February 1984, a group of about 30 guerrillas, including all the members of the Committee of Ten, were shoved with gun barrels of the ANC security into a waiting military vehicle of FAPLA. The tension that had captured the moment was eased when a group of guerrillas inside the closed truck broke out into a song, Akekh' uMandela, usentilongweni, Saze saswel' ikomand' ingenatyala ('Mandela is not here, he is in prison, we have lost a commander'). The trucks and some ANC security officers left for the State Maximum Security Prison in Luanda, where the guerrillas were locked up. The rest of the mutineers in Viana were transported to the two camps of the ANC north of Luanda, Quibaxe and Pango. Once again the Angolan authorities dishonoured the forces of change within the ANC, and added another point in their collaboration to abort a drive to veer the ANC towards democracy.

The mutineers in prison in Luanda were thrown into dark, damp cells with very minimal ventilation. The cells had cement slab beds without mattresses and blankets, and the toilets in the cells were blocked with shit spilling out. The gallery in which the mutineers were held was the one which housed UNITA prisoners, and it had last preference in all prison supplies, including food. Starvation and lack of water was so acute that prisoners were collapsing and dying of hunger and thirst, the only ones surviving being those who were allowed visits from their families and relatives, who even brought them water from their homes.

Several days later, the Commission of Inquiry led by James Stuart [a former trade unionist and ANC stalwart] arrived at the prison. Interviews and recording of statements followed. Five questions were asked:

1. What are the causes of the unrest?
2. What role have you played in the mutiny?
3. Why do you want a national conference?
4. What can you say about the role of the enemy in this?
5. What do you think can be done to improve the state of affairs in the army?

In the process of these interviews, those in prison were joined by

Vuyisile Maseko, who had some head injuries he had received while resisting arrest in one of the ANC centres in Luanda. He had then decided to explode a grenade inside the military vehicle in which he was being transported, which contained also Chris Hani and Joe Modise, who had accompanied a group of security personnel to round up those who had escaped arrest in Viana. Hani and Modise managed to escape unharmed, and in the confusion that ensued Hani issued instructions to the security personnel to shoot Maseko on the spot, but Modise had intervened, saying 'he (Maseko) must go and suffer first'. He had since 'suffered', and was left in prison in Luanda when most of the mutineers were released in December 1988, where he probably still is.

Interrogation and torture in Luanda

The James Stuart Commission concluded its work after more than a week. What followed were interrogations conducted by the security department under two of the most notorious security officers, Itumeleng and Morris Seabelo. These interrogations were conducted not in the way the ANC security was used to. This was because, first, the armed revolts that had surprisingly engulfed the whole army had been characterised by open denunciation of the ANC leadership and a call to investigate the crimes of the security department and Quatro. It was a great shock to the entire leadership of the ANC to learn about their unpopularity within the army. They therefore had to exercise caution in dealing with those arrested so as not to confirm the allegations of atrocities that they were accused of, and they therefore had to restrain their interrogation teams. Second, the Angolan State Security Prison contained a lot of foreigners from different parts of the world, and the Angolan authorities had to make sure that those prisoners did not leave prison confirming the brutalities of the ANC security.

But if you are trained and used to extracting information through beatings and torture, it becomes difficult to sustain a laborious and tedious process of interrogation without falling back to your usual habit. So, here too, they started becoming impatient with this sluggish method, and they resorted to torture and beatings. The prison became more often than not filled with screams from the interrogation rooms as the security personnel began beating up mutineers, hitting them with fists and whipping them with electric cables underneath their feet to avoid traces. Kate Mhlongo, a woman who was a member of the Committee of Ten, had to be hospitalised in the prison wards for injuries sustained under interrogation, followed by Grace Mofokeng, who was also subjected to beatings.

The mutineers decided to take the matter up with the Angolan prison authorities and, in particular, with a Cuban major who was at the top of the prison administration. Promises were made by the prison authorities to stop the torture, but the beatings continued and no action was taken. When Angolan and foreign prisoners began to express their indignation to the authorities about these tortures, beatings and screams, the ANC prisoners decided to take action themselves. In mid-March they embarked on a hunger strike, demanding an immediate end to physical abuses, that they be charged and tried or released immediately, and that President Tambo himself should intervene and understand the political position of the mutineers.

The hunger strike was broken up in its second week when the ANC security took away to Quatro about 11 prisoners, including Zaba Maledza (chair of the Committee of Ten) and Sidwell Moroka. The ANC security complained that Luanda prison was a 'Five Star Hotel' and felt that we were taking advantage of that. They told us that they would take us to 'ANC prisons' where we would never even think of taking any action to secure our release.

The ANC interrogation team was saying that the mutiny was an enemy-orchestrated move to oust the leadership of President Tambo, and they wanted to know who was behind this. They could not accept it as spontaneous, and to confirm that they cited the sudden response of support the mutiny got from all the centres of the ANC in Luanda. Coming out of one of those interrogation sessions in Luanda prison, Zaba Maledza pointed out that the ANC security had decided to frame him up as the one responsible for the whole unrest. They had questioned him about his relationship with Mkhize, the chair of the ANC Youth Section Secretariat, who had paid a visit from Lusaka to Angola shortly before the outbreak. Mkhize had since been deposed from the Youth Secretariat by the NEC.

Later in March, while still in Luanda prison, we were joined by Khotso Morena (Mwezi Twala), who had been in military hospital following an incident in which he had been shot from behind in the presence of Joe Modise and Chris Hani during their round-up of other mutineers. A bullet had pierced through his lung and got out through his front, and he was still in a critical condition. Later still, in April, another three men were imprisoned for their role in the mutiny. The conditions in the prison were worsening and almost everyone was sick, their bodies skeletal and emaciated by lack of food and water. Some began to suffer from anaemia. Their bodies were swollen because of the dampness of the cells, which they were not allowed to leave for exercise or to bask in the sun like the other prisoners. To make things worse, the prison itself had no medicines or qualified medical doctors and all our efforts to appeal to the ANC security personnel to grant us medical treatment, which we knew they could afford better than the Angolan government, were ridiculed. They said the mutineers 'chose to leave the camps, and what was there was only for committed ANC members'.

In that 'Five Star Hotel', Selby Mbele and Ben Thibane lost their lives in a very pathetic way. Selby was speeded to an outside military hospital through the pressure of the mutineers themselves when he was already losing his breath, and he died the same day in the intensive care ward. Ben Thibane was also speedily admitted to an internal prison hospital on a Saturday evening, again through the pressure of his colleagues, at a time when he could hardly walk. In spite of his critical condition, he did not receive any treatment and he lost his life early the following Monday. Both these deaths happened within a space of ten days of each other. With a clear probability of more deaths to follow, the Angolan prison authorities and the ANC leadership were in a state of panic. It was only then that we were allowed, for the very first time, after nine months in that prison, to go out of the dark cells and do some exercises in the sun. Lawrence, a Cuban-trained ANC security official, who coordinated between ANC security and the Angolan prison authorities, for the first time brought us some medicines and even two ANC doctors, Peter Mfelana and Haggar, to examine us. He also brought some food from ANC centres outside.

In February 1985, we received the first visit in Luanda prison from the leadership of the ANC: from Chris Hani, John Motsabi (late NEC member) and John Redi, the director of ANC security. The meeting, which was held in one of the lounges of the Maximum Security Prison, was never fruitful as the guerrillas for the first time levelled bitter criticisms directly at Chris Hani for the treacherous role he had played in suppressing the mutiny. They further called directly on him to stage a public trial of the mutineers.

Hani tried his best to defend his position and announced that the NEC had decided to hold a conference. 'The ANC is committed to justice', he said, and the mutineers would be given a 'fair trial'. He left the prison ashamed of himself. From that time on, Chris Hani, who had managed to win the support of the armed forces before the outbreak of mutiny through false promises, would never even wish to meet with the mutineers on an open platform, except with them as prisoners.

From the Pango revolt to public executions

It will do at this stage to go back a bit, and have a look at one of the bloodiest episodes in the history of MK. This was in Pango camp in May 1984, three months after the suppression of the mutiny and the arrest of the first group at Viana. After the group considered to be the main instigators and ringleaders of the mutiny had been arrested on 16 February, the remaining soldiers at Viana were transported in military vehicles to two camps of the ANC to the north of Luanda, Pango and Quibaxe. These two were the oldest camps of the ANC in Angola and had been evacuated following a mobilisation of the whole army in preparation for the war against UNITA, leaving them with only a few guerrillas to mount their defences. On their arrival, the guerrillas from Viana had to go through interviews with the Stuart Commission. With this over and the commission gone, life began to be tough for the mutineers as the authorities of the camp — composed squarely of those who were loyal to the military leadership — started enforcing castigative rules on people whose emotional indignation at the ANC leadership had barely settled.

A course was introduced arrogantly called 'reorientation'. The political motives behind that were not difficult to know. Mutiny had to be understood as the work of enemy provocateurs, who had been detained, while others had just been blind followers who had fallen prey to their manipulation. The immediate response of the whole group of guerrillas was negative, arguing that their demand for a conference was not disorientation and that they saw no need for the course. Through intimidation, some of the mutineers conformed to pressure to undertake the course but another group refused to comply. It is worth noting that the only people who had weapons in the camp were those loyal to the leadership, and fear and panic had gripped some of the guerrillas about the possible retaliation of the ANC security. Already by that time the security department was conducting interrogations on soldiers, and had been detaining others secretly and sending them to Quatro. The fate of those still in Luanda prison was becoming a concern of everyone, and a serious state of insecurity had set in. This state of insecurity and harassment reached a peak in Pango after some guerrillas had been beaten, tied to trees and imprisoned by the camp security and administration, following an incident in which the camp authorities pointed weapons at a 'culprit' who was between them and the assembled guerrillas.

That Sunday, 13 May 1984, the guerrillas stormed the ANC armoury in Pango camp, disarmed the guards and shot one who refused to surrender his weapon, injuring him. Having laid their hands on the weapons, gun battles ensued throughout the night between the rebel guerrillas and those loyal to the administration of the camp. Zenzile Phungulwa, who was the camp commissar and a staunch defender of the status quo, Wilson Sithole, a staff commissar, Duke Maseko (another loyalist), and a security guard who was guarding prisoners in the camp prison were killed during the fighting that night. The camp commander and other forces loyal to the administration managed to escape and the camp was occupied and run by the mutineers.

The mutineers tried to reach the local authorities of the nearest town to report the matter, but the squad was intercepted by the security forces and after a short battle managed to retreat safely. It became clear then that the ANC commanders had mobilised a crack force of all its loyal cadres in all its camps and establishments in Angola, and they were encircling the guerrilla base. Running battles ensued from five o'clock in the morning the following Friday and continued the whole day as forces under Timothy Mokoena, then a regional commander in Angola and now the army commissar of MK, and Raymond Monageng, then regional chief of staff of MK, arrested in 1988 by the ANC as an enemy plant, struggled to overcome the camp occupied by the mutineers. At dusk that same day the battle ended. About 14 guerrillas were down, and a lot more captured from the side of the mutineers.

Some managed to break out of the encirclement and marched through the bushes further up north. Those captured were subjected to beatings and tortures under interrogation, with melting plastic dripped on their naked bodies and private parts, whipped while tied to trees and forced under torture to exhume the bodies of the ANC loyalists who had died several days before and wash them for a heroic burial. A military tribunal was set up shortly thereafter, headed by Sizakhele Sigxashe, now head of ANC Intelligence, and composed predominantly of security personnel such as Morris Seabelo, a former commander and commissar at Quatro, and at that time chief of security in the whole of the Angola region of MK. Seven men were summarily sentenced to death by public execution by firing squad. They were James Nkabinde (one of Tambo's former bodyguards), Ronald Msomi, Bullet (Mbumbulu), Thembile Hobo, Mahero, Wandile Ondala and Stopper.

Motivated by a genuine desire to democratise the ANC and push it forward to higher levels of armed confrontation for people's freedom, they demonstrated a bravery and a spirit of sacrifice as they walked tall to the firing squad, which shocked even their executioners, not budging an inch from the demand for a national conference and the release of their imprisoned colleagues. Chris Hani, a man who endorsed their execution, was himself forced to comment that 'had this bravery and self-sacrifice been done for the cause of democracy and freedom in South Africa, it would be praiseworthy.' But history teaches us that the jackboot of autocracy knows no limits, and should therefore be opposed limitlessly, starting from wherever you are.

The executed MK soldiers were buried in a mass grave in Pango. Later in the week a group of about 15 who had managed to break through the encirclement of the loyal forces was caught in the province of Uige.

After many days marching through the bush, they had decided to stop at one of the Soviet establishments in the region. After explaining their cause, they requested temporary sanctuary and asked the Soviet officials to inform the Angolan government and the ANC president about the matter. To show that they posed no harm to them and to the local population, they surrendered their weapons to the Soviet-FAPLA authorities. The Soviet officials sent the message to the security department of the ANC, whose personnel arrived in a convoy of military vehicles. The men were surprised in their sleep, tied hand and foot, and under whips, lashings and military boots they were thrown into the trucks, and all the way from there to Pango they were tortured and beaten. In Pango, torture and untold brutalities were unleashed against them, and in the process one of the captured mutineers, Jonga Masupa, died. Others like Mgedeza were found dead in the bushes nearby with bullet holes in them.

The mutineers were kept naked with ropes tied on them for three weeks in the prison at Pango, and any security officer or guards (who had been temporarily withdrawn from Quatro) could satisfy their sadistic lusts on the helpless prisoners. The head of the ANC Women's Section, Gertrude Shope, appeared on the scene from Lusaka at that time and was taken aback by what she saw. She ordered an end to executions and tortures, and that the prisoners

A MISCARRIAGE OF DEMOCRACY 81

should be allowed to get clothes, which was done. Eight of those arrested were taken to Quatro, the rest were given punishments which they served in the camp.

The end of the episode at Pango closed the chapter of armed resistance to enemies of democracy within the ANC. Zaba Maledza, the elected chair of the Committee of Ten, died shortly after these events, on 26 May, in an isolation cell in which he had been kept since 16 February. He was last seen being dragged through the prison with a rope around his neck. The spectre of these young fighters will never stop haunting those who, for fear of democracy and in defence of their selfish interests at the expense of people's strivings for freedom, had nipped their lives at a budding stage.

The Kabwe conference . . . and Quatro

Overwhelmed by shock as a result of the great momentum of the forces for change, the ANC National Executive Committee succumbed. Shortly after the events at Pango, it announced that it had decided to hold a National Consultative Conference the following year, in June 1985. Defensively, ANC leaders rushed to deny that they had been forced to comply with the demands of the mutineers, and that it was the political situation in South Africa that had made them take this decision. Equivocally, they declared that the conference would not be the type of conference that the mutineers had demanded. What did they mean?

In April 1985, two months after Chris Hani's visit to the mutineers in the State Security Prison in Luanda and two months before the National Consultative Conference at Kabwe, in Zambia, 13 mutineers were released from the Luanda prison and one from a group imprisoned in Quatro. Propaganda was whipped up within the ANC membership that those who had been released were innocent cadres who had been misled, and that those remaining in jail were still to be thoroughly investigated. On 12 April, all the remaining mutineers in prison in Luanda were transported to Quatro in handcuffs under a heavy escort of ANC security personnel. What followed, even as the conference proceeded at

Kabwe, was their humiliation and dehumanisation in a place talked about in whispered tones within the ANC.

Quatro was best described in a terse statement by Zaba Maledza, when he said: 'When you get in there, forget about human rights.' This was a statement from a man who had lived in Quatro during one of the worst periods in its history, 1980-82. Established in 1979, it was supposed to be a rehabilitation centre of the ANC where enemy agents who had infiltrated the ANC would be 're-educated' and would be made to love the ANC through the opportunity to experience the humane character of its ideals. Regrettably, through a process that still cries for explanation, Quatro became worse than any prison that even the apartheid regime — itself considered a crime against humanity — had ever had. However bitter the above statement, however disagreeable to the fighters against the monstrous apartheid system, it is a truth that needs bold examination by our people, and the whole of the ANC membership. To examine the history of Quatro is to uncover the concealed forces that operate in a political organisation such as the ANC.

Quatro, officially known as Camp 32, was renamed after Morris Seabelo (real name Lulamile Dantile), one of its first and trusted commanders. He was a Soviet-trained intelligence officer, a student at the Moscow Party Institution and a publicised young hero of the South African Communist Party. In late 1985 he mysteriously lost his life in an underground ANC residence in Lesotho, where none of those he was with, including Nomkhosi Mini, was spared to relate the story.

Located about 15 kilometres from the town of Quibaxe north of Luanda, Quatro was one of the most feared of the secret camps of the ANC to which only a selected few in the ANC leadership (Mzwandile Piliso, Joe Modise, Andrew Masondo and also the then general secretary of the SACP, Moses Mabhida) had access. The administration of the camp was limited to members of the security forces, mostly young members of the underground SACP. Such were most of its administrative staff: for example, Sizwe Mkhonto, also a GDR-Soviet trained intelligence officer and former political

A MISCARRIAGE OF DEMOCRACY 83

student at the Moscow Party Institution, who was camp commander for a long time; Afrika Nkwe, also Soviet intelligence and a politically trained officer, who was a senior commander and commissar at Quatro, with occasional relapses of mental illness; Griffiths Seboni; Cyril Burton, Itumeleng, all falling within the same categories, to name but a few.

The security guards and warders were drawn from the young and politically naive fanatic supporters of the military leadership of Modise and Tambo, who kept to strict warnings about secrecy. They are not allowed to talk to anyone about anything that takes place in an 'ANC Rehabilitation Centre.' The prisoners themselves are transported blindfolded and lying flat on the floor of the security vehicle taking them there. Upon arrival in the camp they are given new pseudonyms and are strictly limited to know only their cellmates, and cannot peep through the windows. From whatever corner they emerge, or any turn they take within the premises of the prison, they must seek 'permission to pass'. Any breaches of these rules of secrecy, whether intentional or a mistake, are seriously punishable by beatings and floggings. To crown it all, when prisoners are being released they must sign a document committing them never to release any form of information relating to their conditions of stay in the prison camp, and never to disclose their activities there or the forms of punishment meted out to them.

The place has seven communal cells, some of which used to be storerooms for the Portuguese colonisers, and five isolation cells, crowded so much that a mere turn of a sleeping position by a single prisoner would awaken the whole cell. With minimal ventilation, conditions were suffocating, dark and damp even in the dry and hot Angolan climate. Even Tambo was forced to comment, when he visited the place for the first time in August 1987, that the cells were too dark and suffocating. In every cell there is a corner reserved for five-litre bottle-like plastic containers covered with cardboard, which serve as, toilet where to the eyes of all cellmates you are expected to relieve yourself. With a strong stench coming from the toilet area and lice-infected blanket rags that stay unwashed for months or even years on end, the prison authorities would keep the doors wide open and perhaps light perfumed lucky sticks before visiting ANC leaders could enter the cells. Outside, the premises of the camp are so clean from the beaten and forced prison labour that again Tambo found himself commenting: 'The camp is very clean and beautiful, but the mood and atmosphere inside the cells is very gloomy.'

In the hands of the SACP

The life activity of the inmates at Quatro is characterised by aggressive physical and psychological humiliation that can only be well documented by the efforts of all the former prisoners and perhaps honest security guards combined. Confronted by questions from the MK combatants before the outbreak of the mutiny, Botiki, one of the former detainees who had lived through camp life in Quatro during its worst period, simply answered: 'What I've seen there is frightening and incredible.'

For a long time, Quatro had been a place of interest to many cadres, and it was difficult to get knowledge of the place from ex-detainees. The ANC security had instilled so much fear in them that they hardly had any hopes that the situation could be changed. The meek behaviour and fear of authority shown by ex-detainees, the intimidative and domineering posture of the security personnel, attempted and successful suicides committed by ex-prisoners such as Leon Madakeni, Mark, and Nonhlanhla Makhuba when faced with the possibility of re-arrest, and the common mental disturbance of the guards and personnel at Quatro, and what they talked about in their deranged state, threw light on what one was likely to expect in this 'rehabilitation centre.'

In Quatro the prisoners were given invective names that were meant to destroy them psychologically, names 'closely reflecting the crimes committed by the prisoners.' Among the mutineers, we had Zaba Maledza named Muzorewa, after a world-known traitor in Zimbabwe; Sidwell Moroka was named Dolinchek, a Yugoslav mercenary involved in a coup attempt in the Seychelles; Maxwell Moroaledi was named Mgoqozi, a Zulu name for an instigator; and there were many other extremely rude names that cannot be written here. Otherwise, generally every prisoner was called 'umdlwembe', a political bandit.

The daily routine started at six with the emptying of toilet chambers, during which prisoners would run down to a big pit under whipping from 'commanders' (security guards) who lined the way to the pits. After this, prisoners would be allowed to wash from a single quarter-drum container at incredible speed. The whole prisoner population was washing from a single container, with water unchanged, taking turns as they went out to dispose of the 'chambers.' The last cells out would suffer most, because they would find water very little and very dirty. The very activity of prisoners washing was a big concession, because before 1985 it was not even considered necessary for the prisoners to wash and they were infested with lice. Each group of prisoners was required to use literally one minute to wash and any delay would lead to serious beatings.

Back to the cell after washing in the open ground, the prisoners of Quatro would be given breakfast which would either be tea or a piece of bread, or sometimes a soup of beans. They were normally given spoiled food that was rejected by the cadres of the ANC in the camps, and it was normally half-cooked by the beaten, insulted and frightened prisoners. The two other meals, lunch and supper, were usually mealie meal and beans, or rice and beans, sometimes in extremely large quantities, which you were forced to eat. To make certain that you had eaten all, there was an irregular check of toilet chambers to detect a breach of this regulation. Alongside the emaciated prisoners there were security guards who lived extravagantly, drinking beer every week, privileges unknown in other ANC establishments. During periods of extreme shortages of food for the prisoners, those who were working would bank their hopes on the left-overs from the tables of the security officers and guards.

Simultaneously with the taking of breakfast, those who wished to visit the medical point would be allowed out. A clinic at Quatro was one of the most horrible places to visit. Usually manned by half-baked and very brutal personnel, a visit to the clinic usually resulted in beatings of sick people and a very inhuman treatment for the prisoners. Errol, one of the mutineers, who had problems with his swelling leg, was subjected to such inconsiderate treatment and beatings whenever he visited the clinic that he finally lost his life. Some prisoners would be forced to go to work while sick, for fear of revealing their state of health that would land them in the clinic. Even reporting your sickness needed a very careful choice of words. For instance, if you had been injured during beatings by the 'commanders', you were not supposed 'to say that you had been beaten. In Quatro, the 'commanders' don't beat prisoners, they 'correct' them: this was the way the propaganda went: 'A prisoner receives a corrective measure.'

After the prisoners had shined the boots of the commanders and ironed their uniforms, at eight o'clock the time for labour would begin. In Quatro there are certain cells that are earmarked for hard and hazardous labour. During this period, the cells predominantly containing mutineers were subjected to the hardest tasks. Lighter duties such as cooking and cleaning the surroundings were given to other groups of prisoners, while the mutineers carried out other work such as chopping wood and cutting logs, digging trenches and constructing dug-outs, and — most feared of all — pushing the water tank up a steep and rough road.

A South African labour process

Every kind of work at Quatro is done with incredible speed. Prisoners are not allowed to walk: they are always expected to be on the double from point to point in the camp. The group that is chopping wood would leave the camp at eight to search for a suitable tree to fell. Everybody had to have an implement, an axe. With work starting after eight, chopping would continue without a break until 12, and you were not even expected to appear tired. 'A bandit doesn't get tired', so goes the saying. Whipping with coffee tree sticks, trampling by military boots, blows with fists and claps on your inflated cheeks (known as 'ukumpompa') became part of the labour process. A work quota you are expected to accomplish is so unreasonable and you are liable to a serious punishment for any failure to fulfil it. Many prisoners at Quatro had their ears damaged internally because of ukumpompa, which was sometimes done by using canvas shoes or soles of sandals for beating the prisoners. The same situation prevailed in other duties. Unreasonably heavy logs for dug-outs had to be carried up the slopes. Every prisoner was cautious to get a piece of cloth for himself to cushion the heavy logs so as to protect his shoulders, but you would still find prisoners doing these duties with patches of bruises incurred through this labour form.

The most feared duty in Quatro was the pushing of the huge water tank, normally drawn by heavy military trucks, by the prisoners themselves for a distance of about three or four kilometres from the water reservoir to the camp. Like cattle, they would struggle with the tank, and the 'commanders' wielding sticks would be around whipping prisoners like slaves whenever they felt like it or when the pace was too slow.

Prisoners in Quatro behaved like frightened zombies who would nervously jump in panic just at the sight of commanders, let alone at a rebuke or a beating. In the process of these beatings during labour time, prisoners who could not cope with the work were sometimes beaten to death. Such was the death of one prisoner who died from blows on the back of his head from Leonard Maweni, one of the security guards. Two others were unable to carry some heavy planks from a place far away from the camp, after the truck that had been carrying them broke down. Upon arrival in the camp they were summoned from their cell, under instructions from Dan Mashigo, who was the camp's chief of staff, and were taken for flogging at a spot near the camp. One never came back to the cell, and the other one died a short while after returning to his cell.

This was in complete conflict with what Dexter Mbona — the security chief in Quatro and later ANC regional chief of security in Angola — told the mutineers when addressing them on their very first day of arrival. On that occasion, he said: 'This camp is not a prison but a rehabilitation centre, and it has changed from what you portrayed it to be during the time of Mkatashingo [the mutiny].'

Quatro was still a place of daily screams and pleas for mercy from physically abused prisoners. Saturday was the worst. It was a day of strip- and cell-searches, The 'commanders' would enter each cell with sticks and the search would commence. At the slightest mistake made by a single prisoner as a result of panic, the whole cell would be in for it, and to drown the noise of their screams, other cells would be instructed to sing.

As already hinted, the whole matter surrounding this camp needs to be investigated to establish who were the masterminds behind these gross violations of human rights. Both psychologically and physically, the camp has done a lot of damage to those who unfortunately found themselves imprisoned there. Some have become psychological wrecks, while other have contracted sicknesses such as epileptic fits: for instance, Mazolani Skhwebu, Hamba Zondi and Mzwandile, three colleagues of the mutineers who were left in Quatro when other members of the group were released in 1988. What is certain is that Andrew Masondo, Mzwandile Piliso and Joe Modise were highly involved in these sinister political machinations. But was the topmost leadership of the ANC unaware? Let justice take its course, and with fairness and honesty let nothing be concealed from the people of South Africa.

From Quatro to Dakawa

Such were the conditions of imprisonment in which the mutineers were held without trial for almost five years, with the sole purpose of breaking their commitment to the democratisation of the organisation they loved. Occasional visits by the leadership of the ANC only served further to frustrate the rebel inmates, to drive them to admit their guilt and to reduce them to tools manipulated by enemy provocateurs. But, if anything, the conditions in Quatro confirmed the justness of their cause and strengthened their commitment to cleanse the ANC of such filth.

The conference on which the detained mutineers had banked their hopes materialised at Kabwe on 16 June 1985, but to their disappointment it never carried out the expected reforms. The

A MISCARRIAGE OF DEMOCRACY

delegation from Angola, the main centre of internal strife, was predominantly composed of selected favourites of the ANC military leadership, who drowned the few who were sent with them as a compromise to give the conference a semblance of representativeness and democracy. The presidential report of O.R.Tambo never even touched the events that had rocked the ANC and led to so much bloodshed, and which had forced the convening of the conference. When the issues behind the mutiny were put on the table by some of the cadres from Angola, the matter was hushed up by Tambo under the pretext that it could divide the ANC. Mr Nelson Mandela had sent a statement to the conference appealing for unity and rallying support for the leadership of Tambo, and it was tactically read at the opening of the conference. It was a further weight against the rebels. Unity, once again, as always, was pushed forward at the expense of a fair and democratic solution of the problems that had beset the ANC. The culprits were saved and further strengthened their positions within the ANC. It was a miscarriage of justice.

Members of the National Executive Committee were to be elected from a list of candidates drafted by Tambo. At the end of the conference we were confronted by our jailers in Quatro and some members of the leadership boasting about unity in the ANC. Our demands for free and fair elections and for an inquiry into the activities and crimes committed by the security apparatus were ridiculed, and they bragged about how isolated the rebels had found themselves in the conference. Pro, one of the camp commanders of Quatro, commented to the mutineers in the cells: 'The people in Lusaka did not even want us to send your lieutenants to the conference, but we insisted here in Angola that they should go, and they experienced bitter isolation when they wanted to raise the disruptive issues of Mkatashingo.' Andrew Masondo was the only one who was sacrificed on the NEC, and that was simply because he was so discredited in Angola that he could not be saved. But the masterminds remained intact.

On 16 November 1988, exactly four years and nine months after the beginning of their imprisonment, the mutineers were summoned to the biggest cell in Quatro. There were about 25 of them in all, and they were required to sign documents committing them to keep the crimes of Quatro a secret. A security officer signed the same documents, as a witness. After an emotional and angry address by Griffiths Seboni, threatening to shoot anyone who repeated anything concerning such problems within the ANC, the rebels were transported to Luanda and kept secretly in a storeroom to avoid contact with MK cadres. [By this time the international negotiations concerning the removal of Cuban troops from Angola were well under way. The removal of the prisoners from Quatro preceded the departure of the bulk of ANC personnel from Angola.]

After two weeks they were secretly taken to the airport and flown to Lusaka, where they were kept in the airport until late at night. The following morning they were transported in an ANC bus to the border between Zambia and Tanzania where, without documents, they were crossed into Tanzania to an ANC Development Centre at Dakawa, near Morogoro. The whole journey took place under the escort of the security personnel and upon arrival in Dakawa they were interviewed by the security officers in one of their bases called the Ruth First Reception Centre.

The main purpose of the interview was for the security officers in Tanzania to check on the mutineers' commitment to what had landed them in prison in 1984. To the disappointment of the security officers, the rebels still justified their cause. Again to the disappointment of the security officers, the welcome they received when they came into contact with the community was unbelievably warm and unique.

The political mood within the ANC in exile had remained shaky since the mutiny of 1984. The divisions between the security personnel and the general membership had continued to widen in spite of cosmetic changes of personnel in the apparatus. Piliso had been shifted from heading security to chief of the Development of Manpower Department (DMD), replaced by Sizakhele Sigxashe, who had been part of the commission set up to probe into the details about the mutiny in 1984. Workshops had also been convened to look into the problems of the Security Department, with the aim of reorganising it in order to change its monstrous face. But these were half-hearted efforts, and could not improve the situation because they evaded the sensitive issues and left out the views of those who had been victims. The old security personnel were, above all, left intact. There was also the pressing issue of the running battles against UNITA that had resumed in 1987, in which MK cadres were losing their lives in growing numbers. Armed struggle inside South Africa, one of the central issues in 1984, was caught up in a disturbing state of stagnation. The leadership of the ANC had become more and more discredited among the exiles, and it was hard to find anyone bold enough to defend it with confidence, as was the case earlier. Even within the security personnel you could detect a sense of shame and unease in some of its members. But it was still difficult for the membership to raise their heads, and the ANC security was in control of strategic positions in all structures.

As a result of this political atmosphere within the ANC, frustration and disillusion had set in at most of the ANC centres. Dakawa, where the ex-Quatro detainees were taken after their release in December 1988, was also trapped in political apathy, with political structures in disarray. The Zonal Political Committees (ZPCs), Zonal Youth Committees (ZYCs), Women's Committees, Regional Political Committees and all the other structures whose membership was elected, were either functioning in semi-capacity or were completely dormant. Only the administrative bodies were in good shape, and this was mainly because their membership was appointed by the headquarters in Lusaka, and was composed of either security or some people loyal and attached to it. These are the structures that, contrary to the ANC policy of superiority of political leadership over administrative and military bodies, wielded great powers in running the establishments and which suffocated political bodies elected by the membership.

This state of affairs reveals clearly that after more than 15 years without democracy and elected structures, the ANC was finding it difficult to readjust itself to the democratic procedures it was forced to recognise by the 1985 Kabwe Conference. The leadership found itself much more at home when dealing with administrators than with bodies that drew support from the grassroots. This strangled political structures, and drove many people away from political concern to frustration and indifference.

Between democracy and dictatorship

When the mutineers arrived in Dakawa, the political mood began to change as they managed to show the people, and those who had taken part alongside them in Mkatashingo, the need to participate and to demand to participate in all issues of the struggle. They themselves took part in all the labour processes of the Dakawa Development Project and showed a sense of keen interest in political matters. When the ANC secretary-general, Alfred Nzo, visited Dakawa shortly after their arrival, he commended their example and called on the community to emulate them. He also announced in the same meeting that the ex-detainees should be integrated into the community and were allowed to participate in all structures. This never excited the ex-detainees, who took it for granted that they were full members of the ANC whose rights were unquestionable, even taking account of the leadership's half-hearted and concealed admissions of past errors, and even if the leadership still did capitalise on the methods used by the mutineers.

With the decision to revive the political structures, a general youth meeting was convened on 18 March 1989 and in the elections a Zonal Youth Committee (ZYC) was elected into office, dominated by former detainees and other participants in the mutiny. Out of its nine members, five were ex-prisoners who had mutinied in 1984, including three members of the Committee of Ten. This initiated the revival of other structures such as the Cultural Committee and the Works Committee (a trade union-like body for labourers in the project) at whose head we had former mutineers. The ANC leadership was clearly eyeing this situation with a sense of discontent, but it was difficult for it to interfere directly with the democratic process under way, without provoking indignation from the community. To them this was a move that absolved the people they had tried to destroy and have ostracised.

The first political encounter between the Dakawa ZYC and ANC headquarters was at the Third Dakawa Seminar, held on 24-25 April 1989. The first and second seminars had been held in 1983 and 1985 respectively and had provided guidelines for the development of the Centre. The objectives of the Third Seminar were to review progress achieved, to establish an autonomous administration for the Centre, to consider new project proposals and to establish proper coordination between the Centre and regional and national structures. The Dakawa ZYC was not invited to be one of the participants. It challenged that decision, and was ultimately allowed to send one delegate, Sidwell Moroka, its chairperson, who was able to deliver its paper.

This paper was prepared after taking stock of the views expressed by the youth meeting of 7 April. Among the participants at the Third Seminar were heads of departments from headquarters including Piliso and Thomas Nkobi, the national treasurer. The paper of the youth of Dakawa was criticised by the leadership. The main theme of the seminar was the need for the setting up of bodies of local self-administration, with the youth pressing for elective bodies and the other side, led by Piliso, dismissing the idea as unrealistic. After lengthy discussions with the chair of the ZYC uncompromising on the issue, Piliso noted that the chairperson of the ZYC was 'stubbornly opposed to appointed personnel.' However, the result was that a recommendation in favour of the position of the ZYC was adopted.

After this seminar, the ANC leadership was to reconsider its attitude towards the former detainees. In June 1989, when the ANC youth section was to attend a World Youth Festival in Korea, a telex was sent to Tanzania from headquarters in Lusaka cancelling the names of four delegates democratically elected by the youth in Dakawa to represent the zone. The four names were all of former mutineers. When an explanation was sought, nobody in the HQ claimed responsibility, but it became clear from discussions between the Dakawa ZYC and Jackie Selebi, chair of the National Youth Secretariat (NYS), that this had the hand of security. The Dakawa ZYC and other upper structures in Tanzania expressed their discontent with this practice that undermined democracy and infringed on the rights of the membership. The Dakawa Youth Committee had by this time already established its Youth Bulletin and was also making its ideas clear in the paper of the whole community, called *Dakawa News and Views*. The local security department and its administrative tools became very uneasy about the articles that began to appear sparing nobody from criticism and with a clear stand for openness and democracy. On several occasions the ZYC found itself a target of attack as instigators, and its office-bearers were intimidated to the point where some of its full-time functionaries, such as Amos Maxongo, were forced to abandon their post. Following a paper prepared by the ZYC in September on 'housing problems in Dakawa', the committee was called to account to the Zonal Political Committee and Administration meeting, and its members were threatened that they should either terminate their contributions in the local newspaper or change their language. The ZYC refused to back away from its position and called for freedom of expression.

This state of political wrangling and the rise in popularity of the Dakawa ZYC approached its climax in September 1989. At this time, the Regional Political Committee (RPC) — a supreme body responsible for political guidance and organisation in different ANC regions — was elected into office in a meeting attended by delegates from all ANC Centres in Tanzania. Sidwell Moroka was elected its chairperson and Mwezi Twala its organising secretary. Both of them were former members of the Committee of Ten elected by the mutineers at Viana in 1984. The closing session, on 16 September, was filled with tension as some of the ANC leading personnel who attended, including Andrew Masondo, Graham Morodi and Willie Williams, and the members of the ANC security, showed clear expressions of disapproval of the results. Morodi, then ANC chief representative in Tanzania, forced himself to occupy the platform and made a comment insinuating that the results should be sent to the NEC for approval. On 18 September he sent a letter to the incoming chair, Sidwell Moroka, suspending accession of the new Regional Political Committee into office with the excuse that he was still awaiting approval from Lusaka. On 5 October the body was dissolved by order of the chief representative, Morodi, who stated that the decision had the backing of the office of the secretary general of the ANC, Nzo. The reasons advanced were that there had been violation of procedures in the meeting and that nominees had not been screened prior to the election, meaning that the ANC security has powers to determine who is eligible for election to the political structures of the ANC. It has a right to dissolve a democratically elected structure if it dislikes those elected by the ANC membership.

Later a body was appointed from ANC headquarters, called the Interim RPC, to replace the democratically elected RPC and to fill the 'political vacuum'. The ZYC circulated a letter in which it disapproved of the imposition of 'dummy structures' and suppression of the democratically elected ones. It further raised the matter at the annual general meeting of the youth on 14 December. Rusty Bernstein, head of the ANC department of political education, and his staff, and the regional chair of the youth, Gert Sibande (that is Thami Mali who was responsible for the 1985 stayaway that rocked Johannesburg), had been invited to attend, and were present. At the annual general meeting, the youth in Dakawa called for the refusal of the personnel appointed to this structure to participate in it. Members of the department of political education and the regional chair of the youth, Sibande, also expressed their disapproval of this undemocratic action and promised to consider their positions in relation to it. This meeting, which Bernstein admitted had shown 'unheard of openness in the ANC', signalled the doom of the Interim RPC, which had until then failed to take office due to its unpopularity and the hesitation of the appointed personnel to play the shameful political role allotted to them. At this point the ANC leadership collected its strength and could not restrain itself any longer.

The destruction of democracy

Under instruction from the NEC, Chris Hani and Stanley Mabizela arrived in Tanzania from the HQ shortly thereafter and called for ANC community meetings in Mazimbu, and on 24 December 1989, in Dakawa. At these meetings, Stanley Mabizela announced the decision of the NEC concerning groups of people who had been imprisoned by the ANC. There were three categories that they mentioned:

1. A group of self-confessed enemy agents who had been imprisoned and released unconditionally. These had a right to take part and even occupy office in ANC structures;

2. A group of enemy agents who had been imprisoned and released conditionally. These had no right to take office in the structures of the movement; and

3. A group of 1984 mutineers who had been imprisoned by the ANC. These were also not allowed to take office in ANC structures. And hence, he concluded, the NEC had decided to dissolve the RPC. He then instructed the communities to support and strengthen the Interim RPC.

This announcement was immediately challenged by the people in the meeting and the former mutineers themselves, with the following arguments:

1. That the National Executive of the ANC was acting autocratically, as it had no moral or political justification for taking a decision so important that it infringed on the right of the membership without even prior consultations with the general membership;

2. That the very issue of the mutiny and the causes behind it had never been opened for discussion by the entire membership of the ANC, and that the mutineers themselves had been denied platforms on which to explain their actions, and that they had never been tried by any court or competent body in the movement; and

3. That the very people who took the decision to dissolve the RPC were still continuing with tortures and murder of detainees and their political opponents.

The last point related to two young men who had escaped from the prison in Somafco at Mazimbu, and who had reported themselves at the Morogoro police station. One of them was Dipulelo, who had headed the *Dakawa News and Views*, and who had been accused of subversion, and detained and tortured by a security department man called Doctor. They arrived at the Tanzanian police station in handcuffs and naked, the way they had been kept in prison at Somafco [where the secondary school principal by this time was Masondo]. They had been detained in July 1989, and they related horrifying stories about the torture to which they had been subjected until they escaped in November.

At the meeting at Dakawa on 24 December, Chris Hani felt he could not tolerate the confrontation and howled from the rostrum at those who challenged the decision. 'The decision is unchallenged, it is an order from the NEC,' he shouted, beating the table with his fist. A commotion ensued as Hani's security tried to arrest those who talked, and a reinforcement of the armed Tanzanian Field Force was called to the hall by Samson Donga. The meeting ended in confusion and the whole community was astonished by the autocratic behaviour of that ANC leadership delegation. On 28 December a paper was circulated, officially banning nine members of different committees in Dakawa. This time again, those who sought the democratisation of the ANC were arrogantly silenced by a decree from the strong opponents of apartheid undemocracy. What an irony!

Resignation from the ANC

Widespread discontent filled the air in Dakawa and it spread to nearby Mazimbu, as the leadership reversed the process of political and cultural renewal that had marked the period in which the ex-mutineers had been free to develop their ideas among the ANC membership. This process of renewal was suppressed, not because there was anything wrong with it but because it threatened the ANC leaders with democracy, which they were not prepared to tolerate. Some members of the department of political education, such as Mpho Mmutle and Doctor Nxumalo, were summoned by the security department and questioned about their association with ex-mutineers, and instructed never again to visit Dakawa. A sense that anything might happen at any time set in, as the community awaited the reprisals that might follow. The whole of the ANC in

Tanzania was filled with tension. From sources close to the security department, word came to the ex-mutineers about meetings held to decide on action to be taken against those who embarrassed the ANC leader and 'the man who wanted to take Mandela's mantle,' Chris Hani.

It was at this time, on 31 December 1989, that the ex-mutineers considered the issue of resigning from the ANC. The reasons are glaring to any realistic-minded person. There was a need to pre-empt the actions of the security department, which would have definitely followed. There was a need also to look for better avenues for continuing the struggle against apartheid, given that the ANC had banned the ex-mutineers from freedom of political expression. And there was also a need to relate this state of affairs to the leadership of the ANC inside South Africa, to the leadership of the Mass Democratic Movement (MDM) and to all the people of South Africa.

We appeal to the People of South Africa and members of the ANC to support our call for an independent commission to investigate these atrocities.

AN OPEN LETTER TO NELSON MANDELA FROM EX-ANC DETAINEES (1990)

Nairobi, Kenya, 14 April 1990

Dear Comrade Mandela,

Revolutionary Greetings!
    The news through the press about our horrific experiences at the hands of the ANC security organs must have left you in a state of bewilderment. Fully aware of that, we realise the need to write you this letter giving an account of our vicissitudes in combating the enemies of democracy within the ANC and putting across also our incessant efforts to have these problems resolved democratically with the full participation of the entire membership. By this we hope to dispel any misunderstandings regarding our decision to expose this disgraceful and shameful page in the history of our organisation, which we hold at high esteem, even at this hour.
    First, it is a fact, undisputable indeed, that the 1984 mutiny was a spontaneous reaction of the overwhelming majority of the cadres of MK to crimes and misdeeds, incompatible with the noble and humane ideals of our political objectives, carried out by certain elements in the leadership of the ANC. These included, among other things, acts of torture and murder through beatings, committed by the ANC Security personnel under the leadership of Mzwandile Piliso; brutal suppression of democracy denying the membership of the ANC any opportunity, for a period exceeding 13 years, to decide

through democratic elections who should lead them; and misleading our people's army by locking it into diversional battles from which our struggle did not benefit, thereby weakening and destroying its fighting capacity.

Second, it remains our firm belief that, had the ANC leadership acted honestly at the very early stages of mutiny, and most of all, had President Tambo responded responsibly to our appeal for his immediate and direct intervention, many lives could have been saved. Regrettably, in a manner identical to our political enemy, the South African regime, the ANC leadership fished out the 'ringleaders' and their most plain-spoken opponents and unleashed virulent brutalities against them.

Third, having gone through close to five years without trial in the most notorious prison within the ANC, and having endured the humiliating, dehumanising and hazardous conditions in which some of us perished, we remained committed to the ANC. This was in recognition of the justness of our cause, in honour of men like you and the multitudes in our beleaguered homeland who languished in racist dungeons and got murdered in this noble cause, and lest we forget our comrades whose lives were cut short by those who deceptively made noise and declarations about democracy on behalf of our people.

Fourth, embarrassed at the way the ANC community in Dakawa absolved us by electing us into the political structures in the Tanzanian ANC region, Chris Hani and Stanley Mabizela, acting on behalf of the National Executive Committee, then muzzled us by banning us from participating freely in ANC political life and dissolving democratically elected structures. Our efforts to challenge such an undemocratic action and to explain the causes of the 1984 mutiny for which we were being unjustifiably treated were answered by shouts from Hani himself, taking us down [from] the platform and even calling for armed Tanzanian Task Force Unit to surround the hall.

It's the realisation of the last-named factor that sealed and shattered our long-standing commitments and hopes to reform the ANC from within, and we resigned in December last year. But let it be stressed still, that even at that time, we limited our activities to consulting the internal leadership of our movement[,] avoiding embarrassing the organisation we so dearly loved. We contacted through letters and attempted to send our document (captured at the Dar-es-Salaam Airport by ANC and Tanzanian security) to such stalwarts of our anti-apartheid struggle as Frank Chikane, General Secretary of SACC, leadership from prison, and Archbishop Desmond Tutu.

Knowing you as a personality who distinguished himself by unflinchingly fighting and standing for human rights and ideals of highest democracy, we receive with bitterness your praises showered at these corrupt and atrocious elements, whilst a shroud of secrecy wraps around the noblest sons and daughters of South Africa who perished in pursuit of the same ideals as yours[,] at the hands of these fake custodians of our people's political aspirations. It is this that pricks our conscience to remove this shroud. Nothing can be more treacherous than to allow such crimes to go unchallenged and unknown. Nothing can be more hypocritical when some of us even at this hour are languishing in those concentration camps.

Even much more disturbing is that these enemies of democracy are to be part of that noble delegation of the ANC to negotiate the centuries-long denied democratic freedoms of our people. What a mockery! What a scorn to our people's sacrifices for freedom! We back your tireless efforts and of all those peace-loving South Africans who see the need for a peaceful settlement of our problems, but we also believe that our people's yearnings for justice can only be competently secured by a morally clean leadership.

We know how difficult it is to accept these bitter but objective truths, and how mammoth the task is of taking appropriate actions against these individuals. But we know also how [undermined ?] they are even within the ANC membership, and we are certain also that, if only they could talk, much more horrific stories will come out of those who tasted the bitterness of the ANC security's treatment. Hence, our sincere call to you and the fighting masses in South Africa and within the ANC to back our demand for a commission to inquire into these atrocities. This, contrary to short-sighted ideas, will not weaken the ANC, but will demonstrate to our people and the world the ANC's uncompromising commitment to justice and democracy. No better guarantee can be made to our people that when our organisation ascends to power, their rights and freedoms will thrive in competent and responsible hands.

Amandla!! NGAWETHU!!
POWER TO THE PEOPLE!!

Yours in the Struggle,
Ex-ANC Detainees

CHALLENGING MANDELA

As Bongani Mkhungo says earlier in this book, when the five ANC fighters returned to South Africa they faced a life of poverty. They and many others had left their schooling or work and gone out of the country to fight for liberation. When they returned they had nothing. Many of their commanders returned at the same time. They soon became parliamentarians or employees of the state. They had won their liberation!

In 1991 Amos Moxongo, one of the Nairobi five, came to Britain to tell people about his experiences. While he was here Nelson Mandela, newly released from prison, also came to Britain and held a press conference. Amos managed to get into the building and afterwards told what happened:

'To Nelson Mandela's deep embarrassment I stood up and told him I was an ex-detainee of the ANC and demanded a commission of inquiry into ANC atrocities against their own fighters. There was consternation among the platform party in Commonwealth House, which included Thabo Mbeki, head of the ANC's international department, Paulo Jordan, of its information department, and Mendy Msimang, chief representative of the ANC in London. So surprised was Mandela by my first question that he asked me to repeat it.

' "I know that the guys who were involved in the 1984 mutiny were innocent", I told him. "If you think otherwise you should prove it to us. You must set a commission of inquiry into the atrocities."

'When he regained his composure, Mandela said that if I still regarded myself as a member of the ANC I should take up my grievances through the structures of the organisation inside South Africa. I told him that I had in fact tried to do so, but had got no response. I added that the matter had been raised with delegates to the recent Johannesburg conference of the ANC — but we didn't know if it had been taken up and we certainly had not had any feedback. At the end of the press conference Mandela sent someone to ask me to go and have a private word with him. I met him in the passage outside the hall. The first thing he said was: "What are you doing in London?"

'I told him that I had come to attend a conference of the International Trade Union Solidarity Campaign. He said: "You should be ashamed of washing the ANC's dirty linen in public." '

This argument against 'washing dirty linen in public' has been used over and over again in movement after movement to stop criticism of bureaucracy, mistaken policies, corruption or, as with the liberation movements in southern Africa, murder and torture. Many people just dismissed these stories of suppression in the liberation movements as 'enemy propaganda'. But even those who had reason to know the stories were true had a great dilemma. It was felt that all those people working against liberation would seize on these reports to discredit the whole liberation movement. When the Namibian twins came to Britain I took them to see a lawyer, a member of an African socialist group in Britain. He had no problem believing their report because his own group had contained a Namibian lawyer who had gone back to Namibia a few years earlier and had herself been accused of being a spy and thrown into a SWAPO jail. The group in Britain had worked through private channels of parliamentarians to get her released. But they had never said anything in public for 'fear of doing damage to the liberation movement'.

Before I went to Kenya to meet the mutineers I met with a union activist in Johannesburg, a member of Workers' Organisation for

Socialist Action, WOSA. He was very interested in the story of the mutiny. He had other information which made him accept that it was true. He asked to meet me on my return to Johannesburg.

In Kenya the ANC mutineers told me they were planning to return to South Africa but they were frightened for their lives. Other ANC members who had fought for democracy, including Chris Hani's former bodyguard Sipho Phungulwa, who had recently returned to South Africa, had been gunned down by MK loyalists. I promised to try and get organisations in South Africa to arrange a reception for the returning Nairobi men to try ensure their safety through maximum publicity for their arrival. But when I got to Johannesburg and met the WOSA member he looked embarrassed. He said he would do what he could but his organisation could not get involved.

Another 'socialist' in Durban asked me why I was so concerned about the activities of the ANC 'security forces' and not the much worse crimes of apartheid. But the real question for me was how could liberation come through movements that themselves suppressed all discussion and resorted to violence against their own members to uphold the 'party line'? What kind of 'liberation' were they after? Whose liberation were they fighting for?

For many people in Britain who have grown up feeling a great sense of solidarity with the struggles in southern Africa, and believing that movements like ANC and SWAPO represented and led those struggles, these accounts will be disturbing. In the past it has been possible for the leading supporters of the liberation movements to sweep all these accounts under the carpet. But now that the masses in eastern Europe have passed a verdict on the 'socialist' Ceauşescu, the 'socialist' Honnecker, and all the rest, it is becoming easier to get a true picture of the 'security' forces in the African liberation movements that they trained. This suppression of democracy took place in all the liberation movements in southern Africa. And the USSR used all of them to put pressure on imperialism as a way of protecting its own interests, in terms of trade deals, bank loans, and so on. Thousands and thousands of young people, students, intellectuals and workers, who wanted to liberate their countries from apartheid or imperialist rule, were lured into a trap. These 'liberation' movements were able to dress themselves up in the cloak of 'socialism' and the Russian revolution, by their association with the USSR. But they were associated, not with the working people of eastern Europe, but with a monstrous bureaucracy that had suppressed every form of working-class democracy and the liberation movements it supported did the same thing in Africa.

When I was in Kenya with the ANC soldiers I showed them the recently published pamphlet by the South African Communist Party leader, Joe Slovo. This pamphlet, *Has Socialism Failed?*, was written in response to the collapse of the regime in Moscow. In it he says that whatever else went wrong in eastern Europe, the fact remains that the liberation movements know that these regimes supplied them with arms. The ANC fighters laughed and said: 'Yes, but what were the guns used for?'

This account of the mutiny details the way that the Cuban and Angolan forces were used to suppress the people fighting for democracy. The full meaning of this was made clear in 1994 when an Angolan refugee in London, a member of the African Liberation Solidarity Campaign, gave this account of her experiences in the 'liberation' struggle in Angola.

Bob Myers
June 1997

'NOBODY COULD WALK FREE'
AN ANGOLAN WOMAN'S STORY
(1994)

An Angolan woman tells here of the bloody terror unleashed on her people by the Stalinist-backed ruling MPLA (Popular Movement for the Liberation of Angola, now the ruling party) following Angola's declaration of independence in 1975. At that time the author was a 16-year-old schoolgirl. Her account of the MPLA's activities throws a grim light on the role of Stalinism, especially in Africa. It was Stalinism that was responsible for similar brutal killings of freedom fighters in Namibia and South Africa. For obvious reasons, the author's name cannot be revealed.

In 1974 the workers of Portugal rose up and removed the despotic, fascist regime in their country. By this act they also removed Portuguese imperialist rule from the backs of the Angolan working people. And so, in 1975, we celebrated Independence Day.

For many years before that the mass movement in Angola had been prepared by many underground groups and committees organised in the factories and in every sector of the population. I was a 16-year-old schoolgirl, and active on a committee called Amilcar Cabral. Everyone was involved in one way or another — nobody stood aside. It was a massive movement. On Independence Day everybody came out into the open.

But already in the liberation struggle the agencies of the superpowers — the US and the USSR — had moved in. The conditions were already there for the Soviet Stalinist bureaucracy to take over the MPLA, as it was the main source of its weaponry, finance and all other supplies. The other liberation movements, the FNLA (National Front for the Liberation of Angola) and UNITA (National Union for the Total Independence of Angola), got their support from the US. The division was clear: imperialism on one side and the perpetrators of terror against the people in the name of socialism, the Stalinist bureaucracy, on the other. Both acted only in their own interests — to ensure that their power bloc was protected and enlarged. The thousands of freedom fighters, the workers, the peasants, and the young, could be starving, sick, homeless, wounded and forced to flee their homes — that did not bother them.

Naturally the vast majority of the people chose the MPLA, and were proud that the USSR — which embodied the great cause of socialism — was giving its support. In those days our understanding of Stalinism was not so clear.

The FNLA and UNITA marched on the capital, Luanda, and there was a battle with the MPLA forces, which were victorious. Throughout Africa and the world, including Angola, the workers and peasants hailed the new government of Marxist-Leninists. But what was the truth? Within the MPLA there was conflict.

For years, it was the leaders of the armed struggle within the country who had had the main influence on the people. Now many leaders were returning from exile, and it was they who became the ministers in the new government under Agostinho Neto, the president.

Most Angolans thought that the great Soviet Union would help their country overcome its economic and other problems, that there could now be a peaceful transition to democracy and socialism. But this was not the role played by the leaders of the Soviet Union. Instead they exacerbated the differences in the MPLA, and advised the government to clamp down on the people. Instead of encouraging the mass movement, and all the committees that had been built throughout the country during the liberation struggle, they acted to behead this mass movement.

First they stopped the right to strike. The first people to be put in prison were the leaders of the main textile factories in Luanda. Then the students were dealt with: their leaders were imprisoned. By 1976 the situation had become really volatile.

The three most radical groups of committees — Amilcar Cabral, Active Revolt and Henda Committees — realised that the main question was how to build the vanguard party. We were well known throughout the mass movement, but we needed to consolidate the vanguard workers and students into such a vanguard party. Everyone agreed that a real communist party had to be built, one that had its roots in the mass movement and was not the servant of the authoritarian Soviet bureaucracy.

We founded the Angola Communist Organisation to organise opposition throughout the mass movement. We were very successful. The MPLA had one government-run newspaper, but we had at least six newspapers. We were young and naïve. We were exhilarated by independence, and we thought we could build a socialist future. We had no idea about what would happen.

We came under attack. Our papers were closed down. Those who were not imprisoned continued the fight. There was unrest and revolt among the whole population. The people were looking for some alleviation of their hard lives. This put pressure on the warring factions in the MPLA leadership.

Nito was leader of one faction, and those in the other, who were closest to President Agostinho Neto, had been educated and trained by the Stalinist bureaucracy during their years of exile. Nito was much younger and he had been fighting inside the country. But neither of these factions had the interests of the working people at heart. Both were trying to prove to the leaders of the USSR that they were their most reliable allies to contain and defeat the mass movement.

Nito was the interior minister and was responsible for the security forces, which were attacking any action by the workers, peasants and students. He thought that he had the support of the USSR when in May 1977 he and his faction, supported by the armed forces, carried out a coup. On the night before this action, Nito told me that he had had discussions in the Soviet and Cuban embassies and they were supporting him. He had assured them that he would allow the president to remain in office, but arrest other government ministers.

Nito's forces took over the national radio and television stations and the main political prison, and arrested members of the government. Thousands of people were already marching in the streets and on the government building. The people thought they would get a government that would really represent their interests — a government composed of those who had been in the forefront of the armed struggle for liberation. But the leaders of the USSR had other ideas.

They broke their agreement with Nito. On 27 May 1977, tanks — commanded by the Cubans — were on the streets to defeat the coup. The masses of people around the national radio station were fired on and many were killed.

The link between the president and the Soviet leadership was Lara, who had already come back from exile in the Stalinist camp. He was the political organiser of the MPLA. Both factions in the power struggle were Stalinist, but the bureaucracy in the USSR knew that Neto, Lara, and other MPLA leaders who had also lived in exile, such as Iko and Onambwa, were completely in their hands. Nito had to run for his life. He lived in the bush until he was finally arrested and killed.

A clean-up operation started in the city. From then onwards anyone who spoke against the MPLA was imprisoned and killed. It was impossible to speak. There was no free speech, no public meetings. People were arrested on the spot. Many thousands died — it was worse than anything known under the old colonial rule. On the border with Namibia people were thrown off the mountains to be eaten by the lions. Fear overtook everyone.

Nito was handed over by the population. Even inside your own family, your own home, you were never secure. Lara boasted that, after the defeat of the coup and the clean-up of the mass movement, the MPLA would not have to worry about any opposition for another 20 years.

They were secure — all opposition was eliminated. Anyone who showed the slightest opposition to the MPLA government was taken away and killed. And all this was carried out under the supervision of the Soviet Union through the army, the government, and the security forces. Advisers from the Soviet Union, east Germany, Cuba, Bulgaria and Romania ruled the country. Even methods of torture, of tracking people down, and of making people speak were the methods and techniques perfected by Soviet intelligence — the KGB. The security forces were trained by Cuban intelligence and the KGB. We were all overwhelmed by the scale of the repression.

None of us was prepared for this. My sister was arrested. Her husband was arrested and killed. My sister was not even political — she was a housewife and mother of two children, who were one and two years old at the time. On the day they arrested my sister, they left these two children completely on their own in the house.

And the state never acknowledged the deaths of the people they killed — they were just 'missing'. Many were incarcerated in the notorious Estrada de Catete, a prison near Luanda built by the Cubans. It is the worst prison you could imagine. The cells are below ground level, so the prisoners feel they are buried alive. The regime is barbaric and the conditions are inhuman.

My sister was in Casa da Reclusão prison. When I visited her I saw South African and Namibian prisoners there. And we heard that they were from the liberation struggles in those countries. When I first visited my husband his face was bruised, bloody and swollen. He was covered in blood. We visitors were helplessly trying to wipe the blood off our loved ones.

I was not in prison, but life was terrible. There were threatening telephone calls from the security forces. I was followed and checked everywhere. I nearly committed suicide. That was when two security men came to my home. They were brutal, rude and arrogant. They took food and drink from the cupboard and sat at the table talking and laughing loudly.

They asked me: 'What does a nice young woman like you do now that your husband is in prison?' I knew what was to come. They grabbed me and threatened to rape me. I fought as hard as I could. My face was all bruised and swollen. Then they said that they wouldn't even think of touching me themselves, but would use their revolver inside me. I tore myself away and rushed to the balcony of the flat to jump out and kill myself. Luckily for me a crowd of neighbours appeared and the security men backed off.

Finally I had to leave the country five years ago because the security forces found papers implicating me in the opposition. In fact we did everything we could to secure certain archives because we knew that sooner or later we would need to write this history. But I do not know whether these will ever be retrieved.

In 1978 the mothers and wives joined together to ask where were their sons and husbands. President Neto began to feel the pressure of this. After the coup he had made a speech on television, saying that those involved in the coup would be shown no mercy. Some of the families received death certificates. But the majority did not even have the deaths confirmed. My sister still has no death certificate for her husband; according to the Angolan states she is still married to him. It is a very difficult thing to live with. Her children are now 18 and 19 years old.

In 1979 Neto died. There were many rumours surrounding his death. Some say that the USSR needed to remove him because he was 'going soft'. He died on a hospital operating table — he was not an old man, only in his fifties. At the time of his death Neto appeared to be trying to change some of the policies within the country.

There was some talk of amnesty for prisoners. Neto had started visiting different parts of the country, and seemed to be retreating from his hard line. The new president, Dos Santos, was appointed from within the MPLA. He is a man in the true Stalinist mould. He is president of everything, and the MPLA controls everything — the state, the party, the lives of everybody. Dos Santos is even president of the peasants' association, the women's association, and the writers' organisation, and he is commander-in-chief of the armed forces and every other department of state. This kind of bureaucratic centralisation of the government means that the country has become paralysed.

It is impossible to do anything. You must get the president's signature for everything. If he doesn't sign, then nothing happens. The functioning of the state is frozen. The economy is paralysed. All funds are used to buy arms from Russia, while the people starve, are homeless, are without hospitals, schools and even the most basic necessities of life, and everybody lives in fear.

Dos Santos, on the basis of his organising support for the liberation struggles of the South West Africa People's Organisation in Namibia and the African National Congress in South Africa, won the support of the working class in the African countries and internationally. The main question was to get rid of the system of apartheid. Anyone who was in the front line of that battle won support from the workers. But behind this smokescreen, and under the leadership of the Soviet Stalinist bureaucracy, the MPLA government was carrying out atrocities against the people of Angola. In the 1970s and immediately after independence, UNITA was almost finished — the MPLA had the people's full support. Now, after such repression, many Angolans started to support UNITA, even though it was organised and led by their enemies — the apartheid capitalist government of South Africa and world imperialism.

In the main battle in the post-independence civil war, at Kuito Kuanavale, the Cuban-backed MPLA fought it out with the South African-backed UNITA. Thousands of young Angolans were killed. At the end of the battle the MPLA had to abandon the fight, and UNITA was left in control of the area. Thousands of young South Africans and Cubans also died.

The Stalinist bureaucracy and the Cuban leadership, together with the Stalinist leadership of the MPLA, are to blame for UNITA's resurgence, and for the bloody war that continues in Angola. But by the mid-1980s the mass movement was again coming forward — this time for peace. Everybody was tired of the war. Luanda had been under siege for almost 16 years.

There had been a curfew in the city ever since Independence Day! Nobody could walk free. Life was not normal. The social infrastructure has been almost completely destroyed, including the hospitals and schools. People are dying without treatment. Hospitals are now places to go, not for treatment, but just to die. The schools are running out of any kind of support — there are no books and even no chairs for the children to sit on. There is no electricity in most areas. There is a marked difference between the huge complex around the oil wells, which have their own generators and are flooded with light, and the villages where the poor people live, which are in total darkness.

I was a teacher. It was terrible. The children came to school without having had anything to eat. They would sit there with dry mouths, and that awful gaze in their eyes. They would just sit there and then fall down. Starvation is taking its toll everywhere. The markets have closed because there is nothing to sell. The only way to buy anything is on the black market. But that is extensive and the wages of those who are lucky enough to have work are very low. A worker could probably buy one fish with his or her monthly wage. The huge gap between low pay and the cost of black-market goods has increased corruption. Everybody has to live by buying and selling something. The MPLA, which was hailed by the masses during the liberation struggle, has now become the party which centralises everything that is corrupt and rotten. It has become a means of survival in the very worst way. Everybody tries to get into party positions, local government and state jobs. There are special shops selling to the party élite goods not generally available. Everybody needs to belong to the party because only by being a member can anybody get anything. If you want your children to get reasonable schooling, with a teacher actually there, then you can only get it if you are in the party. Everything has a price. If you want documents and papers stamped and signed, you must pay.

If you are 'lucky' enough to have a state or local government job, then you are in the business of taking money for such signatures and stamps, but the whole population is not in the party, and so one in ten of the people is a refugee within their own country. All the hopes of the people for revolution, for socialism, have been completely destroyed.

Many of the prisoners who were released in the 1980s were so disturbed that they could not cope with life outside. A close friend and comrade of mine committed suicide in front of his family — he set light to himself. I could give you many examples of such tragedies. But, even with all this destruction, the voice of the workers can be heard. There are strikes of teachers and hospital workers.

And the oil workers of Angolan nationality went on strike because, even though they are a privileged section of the working class, they were not getting the same wages and conditions as the oil workers in the multinationals from Britain, France and the US. Workers in the Soviet Union fought for their rights and have now changed the whole situation there.

The Stalinist bureaucracy can never again present the USSR and eastern Europe as being socialist, or themselves as leading the world's working class towards socialism. They can never again dupe people into believing that they are Marxist-Leninists. Their puppets in the MPLA, in SWAPO, and in the ANC stand exposed.

Now we must build the real international workers' party. There is one last thing, and it has to do with the way we must build this international workers' party. Even though I have explained that the Cuban tanks and advisers were used against the Angolan workers, peasants and students, I believe that Cuba and the gains that were won against imperialism must be defended.

REBUILDING THE INTERNATIONAL REVOLUTIONARY MOVEMENT

Widespread suppression of the youth, of intellectuals, and of militant trade unionists, as reported in this book, had one purpose — to stop a struggle against capital. The working masses and peasantry could be used as a battering ram against white rule or colonial rule to secure a good grain deal for the USSR or a place at the rich men's table for the black African bourgeoisie but the masses could not be allowed to find their own voice and fight for their own interests, for their own liberation.

As long as the Soviet Union was ruled by bureaucrats who suppressed any working-class activity in their own country, the African bourgeoisie could freely dress their liberation movements up as socialist. The millionaire ANC member and the unemployed youth could both be called 'comrade' and could both talk about the 'struggle' for 'liberation'. The Namibian detainees were tortured in the 'Marxist School of Education'. There was no one to speak out against this fraud.

But once the regimes in eastern Europe collapsed this borrowing of 'socialist' camouflage for the African bourgeoisie becomes increasingly difficult. Like their masters they are all becoming free marketeers. They now preach liberation through privatisation and International Monetary Fund plans.

All the accounts in this book deal with the period when the old world order was breaking down. The collapse of the regimes in eastern Europe and the growing crisis within the capitalist system internationally open up not a 'new world order', as the imperialists would like to believe, but a 'world disorder', a world in which the working class is freed from the kind of tyranny dressed up as 'socialism' that dominated the liberation movements and the working-class movements around the world. It is possible to begin to rebuild a liberation movement, a movement to transform society, that can act in the interests of the majority of the people, not in the interests of the few.

The second book in this series, *Is this really what we fought for?*, reprints a number of pamphlets produced by Bongani Mkhungo and other workers in the Durban area as they have worked to win the trade unions back from the bureaucrats and to build a revolutionary movement to put an end to the misery created in Africa by capital's exploitation and domination of human beings.

Bob Myers
June 1997